CW01372121

2024
PARIS
OLYMPICS

2024 OLYMPIC SPORTS

GUIDE TO PARIS

Copyright © 2024 A&D PUBLISHING

All rights reserved. No part of this publication may be reproduced, distributed, or transmitted in any form or by any means without the prior written permission of the publisher, except in the case of brief quotations embodied in critical reviews and certain other noncommercial uses permitted by copyright law.

ISBN: 979-832-858-070-0

Table of Contents

- ARCHERY 7
- ARTISTIC GYMNASTICS 8
- ARTISTIC SWIMMING 10
- BADMINTON 11
- BASKETBALL 12
- BASKETBALL 3X3 13
- BEACH VOLLEYBALL 14
- BOXING 15
- BREAKING 17
- CANOE SLALOM AND SPRINT 18
- CYCLING BMX FREESTYLE 20
- CYCLING BMX RACING 21
- CYCLING MOUNTAIN BIKE 22
- CYCLING ROAD 23
- CYCLING TRACK 24
- DIVING 27
- EQUESTRIAN 28
- FENCING 29
- FIELD HOCKEY 31
- GOLF 32
- HANDBALL 33
- JUDO 34
- MARATHON SWIMMING 36
- MODERN PENTATHLON 37
- RHYTHMIC GYMNASTICS 38
- ROWING 39
- RUGBY SEVENS 41
- SAILING 42
- SHOOTING 45
- SKATEBOARDING 47
- SOCCER / FOOTBALL 48
- SPORT CLIMBING 49
- SURFING 50
- SWIMMING 51
- TABLE TENNIS 54
- TAEKWONDO 55
- TENNIS 57
- TRACK & FIELD / ATHLETICS 59
- TRAMPOLINE GYMNASTICS 70
- TRIATHLON 71
- VOLLEYBALL 72
- WATER POLO 73
- WEIGHTLIFTING 74
- WRESTLING 76
- REFERENCES 78

The 2024 Games are scheduled to take place from July 26 to August 11. Over the span of nineteen days, 329 events will unfold, with contestants from 206 countries competing for medals. Around 10,500 athletes are expected to participate in more than 750 sporting sessions. The official start date is Friday, July 26, with the Games concluding on Sunday, August 11. However, soccer and rugby competitions will kick off on July 24, followed by the handball tournament on the 25th.

ARCHERY

Olympic archery contests will take place between July 25 and August 4 at *Les Invalides* in Paris. It comprises five events: individual competitions for women and men, team competitions for women, and men and a mixed event.

All disciplines are set to feature *recurve* archery competitions, held under the 70 meter approved distance and rules. This implies that the targets, measuring 122 centimeters in diameter, are placed 70 meters from the contestants. The archers' objective is to shoot their arrows as accurately as possible towards the center of the target to surpass their opponents. It's worth noting that the only type of bow allowed to be used at Olympic level is the *recurve* bow. A *recurve* bow is characterized by limbs that curve away from the archer when unstrung, which helps store more energy and provides greater power and accuracy to the arrow when the bow is drawn and released. The sport of archery demands intense concentration and dexterity from its competitors. Archers must effectively manage their nerves, as a single mistake can prove costly, particularly in duels at the finals and in individual events.

128 archers (64 for each gender) will compete across the **five medal events**:
- women's team finals on Sunday, July 28 at 17:11
- men's team finals on Monday, July 29 at 17:11
- mixed team finals on Friday, August 2 at 16:43
- women's individual finals on Saturday, August 3 at 14:46
- men's individual finals on Sunday, August 4 at 14:46

Archery, the use of bow and arrows, developed alongside human civilization, initially for hunting and warfare. Ancient or classical civilizations such as the Akkadians, Assyrians, Egyptians, Nubians, Greeks, Persians, Romans, Indians, Koreans, Chinese, and Japanese are known to have fielded archers in their armies. Some of the earliest recorded archery tournaments took place during the Zhou dynasty (1027- 256 BC) in China. Archery was an important military and hunting skill throughout classical antiquity and the medieval period, until it was eventually replaced by firearms.

Archery was featured in the modern Olympics in two different periods. The sport made its debut at the Olympics held at Paris in 1900. It was contested again in 1904, 1908, and 1920, but was dropped from the program because there were no internationally recognized rules for the sport and each Games through 1920 held a different type of event. With the creation of the International Archery Federation in the 1930s, a set of international rules were created. However, it was not until 1972 that archery was reintroduced at the Games in Munich with women's and men's individual events. Both team events were included in the program at the 1988 Seoul Olympics, while the mixed team event was added in the 2020 Tokyo Games. Since its return to the Olympics in 1972, South Korea has emerged as the dominant force in archery, securing over half of the available gold medals, with 27 out of 45.

ARTISTIC GYMNASTICS

The artistic gymnastics competitions in 2024 will take place between the July 27 and August 5 at the Bercy Arena in Paris.

Artistic gymnastics is a discipline that involves performing choreographed routines on various apparatus, demonstrating strength, flexibility, agility, and grace through a series of acrobatic movements, jumps, flips, and dance elements. It is composed of a number of individual events on different apparatus, as well as an all-around competition involving all of them. There is also a team contest that includes performing routines on all apparatus.

During Olympic tournament, gymnastics meets are divided into multiple sessions held on various days: qualifications, team finals, all-around finals, and event finals.

In the qualification round, gymnasts compete alongside their national squad on all four (for women) or six (for men) events. The scores from this qualifying session are not used to award medals; instead they are utilized to determine which nations progress to the team finals and which individual athletes qualify for the all-around and apparatus finals. Each country can have a maximum of two gymnasts advancing to each event final, as well as the all-around finals.

During the team finals, gymnasts compete with their national squad on all four (for women) or six (for men) events. The scores from this session determine the medalists in the team competition.

In the all-around finals, athletes compete individually across all four (for women) or six events (for men), and their combined scores establish the allocation of the medals in the all-around competitions.

During the event finals or apparatus finals, medals are contested by the top eight gymnasts on each apparatus, determined by their scores in the qualification round.

Each discipline requires different skills. Men compete across the floor exercise, pommel horse, rings, vault, parallel bars and horizontal bar, whereas women's events comprise the vault, uneven bars, balance beam, and floor exercise. From dynamic sequences to intricate compositions, these elements necessitate strength, agility, coordination, and precision, each more spectacular than the last.

In contrast to the branches of many other sports, men's and women's artistic gymnastics feature notable differences in both technique and the apparatuses used during competitions.

Until 2004, gymnastics routines were evaluated with a maximum score of 10 points. Starting from 2005, the scoring system changed to a combination of a D-score (reflecting skill requirements, difficulty value and connection value – for skills performed back to back with no pause in between) and an E-score (evaluating execution and artistry). This change aimed to provide greater differentiation between athletes' performances. While the maximum E score remains 10, there is no limit to the D score. Theoretically, this implies that scores could be infinite. However, average scores for routines in major competitions have generally been in the low to mid teens.

The sport started to consider making changes to the scoring system after the 1976 Montreal Games, where Romanian gymnast Nadia Comăneci achieved the first-ever 'perfect score' of 10.

The artistic gymnastics program for Paris 2024 will feature **fourteen events** in total (eight for men and six for women):
- men's team finals on Monday, July 29 at 17:30
- women's team finals on Tuesday, July 30 at 18:15
- men's individual all-around finals on Wednesday, July 31 at 17:30
- women's individual all-around finals on Thursday, August 1 at 18:15
- men's floor exercise finals on Saturday, August 3 at 15:30
- women's vault finals on Saturday, August 3 at 16:20
- men's pommel horse finals on Saturday, August 3 at 17:10
- men's rings finals on Sunday, August 4 at 15:00
- women's uneven bars finals on Sunday, August 4 at 15:40
- men's vault finals on Sunday, August 4 at 16:25
- men's parallel bars finals on Monday, August 5 at 11:45
- women's balance beam finals on Monday, August 5 at 12:36
- men's horizontal bar finals on Monday, August 5t at 13:31
- women's floor exercise finals on Monday, August 5 at 14:20

The practice of gymnastics has been mentioned in ancient writings and was recommended by Greek philosophers as a way of combining physical exercise with intellectual activity. Its ancient origins emphasize its longevity as a sport. Initially it included many disciplines, several of which later became separate sports. Gymnastics was also used for military training.

Modern gymnastics, as we know it, began to take shape in the early 19th century. The term *artistic gymnastics* emerged to distinguish the freestyle performances from those used in military training. Friedrich Ludwig Jahn, a renowned German educator often hailed as the father of gymnastics, pioneered various apparatuses, including the horizontal bar, parallel bars, rings, and the pommel horse. The sport grew in popularity over the course of the 19th century, with an increasing number of competitions.

Gymnastics was introduced at the very first Olympic Games of the modern era in 1896, and has been included in every edition since, but female gymnasts were not allowed to participate in the Olympics until 1928. The artistic gymnastics schedule evolved a lot from the first half of the 20th century, before it was settled in 1936 for men and in 1960 for women.

In the 1960s and 70s, Japan dominated the Olympic podium, before being surpassed by the Soviet Union and East Germany. Nowadays, center stage in artistic gymnastics is primarily occupied by Japan, USA, Russia, and China.

In the men's overall count, Japan won the most medals, totaling 101 (33 gold, 34 silver, and 34 bronze). Meanwhile, the Soviet Union clinched the highest number of golds, with 39 out of their 94 total medals. In the women's medal standings, the former Soviet Union leads with 88 medals (33 gold, 29 silver, and 26 bronze), followed by Romania with 62 medals (24 gold, 16 silver, and 22 bronze), and the USA with 54 medals (16 gold, 22 silver, and 16 bronze).

ARTISTIC SWIMMING

Artistic swimming (formerly called *synchronized swimming*) consists of two events: a duet and a team competition. Each event includes a free and a technical routine, with the acrobatic routine being added to the team competition in 2024. The athletes perform in a 3-meter deep, 25-meter long, and 20-meter wide pool.

Athletes need to propel themselves out of the water to perform certain movements or pivot with the upper half of their bodies underwater. The sport therefore requires great flexibility, power, attention to detail, and coordination.

There will be three major changes to artistic swimming at 2024 Games:
- The acrobatic routine has been added to the team competition (along with the free and technical routine)
- Teams can include two male swimmers (for the first time in Olympic history in the team event)
- A new scoring system will be applied in Paris, which is only new to the Olympics since it has already been used at the 2023 world championships in Fukuoka.

In the new scoring system, two main criteria are used to evaluate a routine: execution and artistic impression. Both have almost the same importance in terms of how they impact the score. The introduction of this system aims to reduce subjectivity in evaluating artistic swimming routines by establishing a more standardized judging process. It also makes the competition more exciting, firstly because the results are now unpredictable, but also because coaches now have more strategic input.

A number of 96 swimmers will compete at the Aquatics Center across **two medal events**:
- team technical on Monday, August 5 at 19:30
- team free on Tuesday, August 6 at 19:30
- team acrobatic on Wednesday, August 7 at 19:30 – with medals awarded
- duet technical on Friday, August 9 at 19:30
- duet free on Saturday, August 10 at 19:30 – with medals awarded

At the turn of the 20th century, artistic swimming or synchronized swimming was known as *water ballet*. The first recorded competition took place in 1891 in Berlin, Germany. Many swim clubs emerged during that period and the sport also gained momentum in Canada. As well as existing as a sport, it frequently served as a captivating feature in Music Hall evenings, where on-stage water tanks were installed specifically for this purpose.

Artistic swimming became an Olympic discipline at the Los Angeles 1984 Games. From 1984 through 1992, the Olympics featured solo and duet competitions, but they were both dropped in 1996 in favor of team competition. At the 2000 Sydney Games, the duet competition was restored and is now featured alongside the team competition. Traditionally, the United States, Canada, and Japan have been the strongest nations in the sport, winning the Olympic medals from 1984 through 1996, but Russia has recently dominated, winning every event between 2000 and 2020.

BADMINTON

The badminton tournaments at the 2024 Paris Games are scheduled to run from July 27 to August 5 at *La Chapelle* Arena. Olympic badminton has five events: women's singles, men's singles, women's doubles, men's doubles and mixed doubles.

Badminton is a sport played using rackets, to hit a shuttlecock, a conically shaped projectile with a crown of feathers, across a net. It is competed by either two opposing participants (singles) or two opposing pairs (doubles). Badminton is frequently played as a leisurely activity outdoors in a yard or on a beach, but competitive matches are contested on a rectangular indoor court.

In each game, participants aim to reach 21 points, earning a point for every rally they win. If the score ties at 20–20, the game continues until one side gains a two-point lead, except when there is a tie at 29–29, in which case the game goes to a golden point of 30. The winner of this rally will clinch the game. Matches are best out of three: a player or pair must win two games (of 21 points each) to win the match.

At high levels of play, badminton demands excellent fitness: players require aerobic stamina, agility, strength, speed, and precision. In addition to being a technical sport, it calls for good motor coordination and the development of sophisticated racket movements that require much greater wrist flexibility than other racket sports.

A total of 172 badminton players (86 for each gender), will compete across **five medal events**:
- mixed doubles finals on Friday, August 2 at 16:10
- women's doubles finals on Saturday, August 3 at 16:10
- men's doubles finals on Sunday, August 4 at 16:10
- women's singles finals on Monday, August 5 at 10:55
- men's singles finals on Monday, August 5 at 15:40

Badminton evolved from the earlier game of battledore (an older term for racket) and shuttlecock, although its precise origins remain uncertain. One plausible theory is that it was played at the stately home of the Duke of Beaufort in Gloucestershire sometime in the early 1860s and thus was named after his estate, which was called Badminton House. It is not known exactly when battledore and shuttlecock transitioned into badminton, but the sport gained traction in British India, where it became very popular by the 1870s, particularly among expatriate officers in military cantonments. From there, its popularity gradually spread to other British colonies and eventually to Europe and East Asia.

Badminton was first introduced as a demonstration sport during the 1972 Games in Munich. In 1988, it was displayed as an exhibition event in Seoul. Finally, it debuted as an official sport in the 1992 Barcelona Games, featuring four medal categories: women's and men's singles and women's and men's doubles. The mixed doubles category was added four years later at the Atlanta Games. Throughout Olympic history, athletes from Asian nations have dominated so far the medal standings, accounting for 106 out of the 121 medals awarded.

BASKETBALL

The basketball tournaments for the 2024 Olympics are scheduled from July 27 to August 11. Preliminary matches will take place at Pierre Mauroy Stadium in Lille, with the final phase staged at the Bercy Arena in Paris.

Basketball is competed by two opposing teams of five players on a rectangular, indoor court. Participants utilize their hands to control the ball, aiming to score points by successfully throwing it through the defender's hoop – a basket 18 inches (46 centimeters) in diameter mounted 10-feet (3.048-meter) high to a backboard at each end of the court – while preventing the opposing team's attempts to score through their own hoop.

Olympic basketball games consist of four 10-minute quarters. The time allowed is actual playing time; the clock is paused while play is not active. Therefore, games generally take much longer to complete than the allocated game time. A field goal is worth two points, except when scored from behind the three-point line, where it counts for three. When a foul occurs, timed play stops and the player fouled or designated to shoot a technical foul is given one, two or three one-point free throws. The team that accumulates the highest score at the end of the game emerges victorious. In the event of a tie, when regular play concludes, an extra period (overtime) is conducted to determine the winner.

Players advance the ball by bouncing it while walking or running (dribbling) and by passing it to a teammate, both of which require considerable talent. They must demonstrate endurance, flexibility and, of course, a great deal of skill as they run up and down the court and shoot baskets.

A total of 24 teams (12 women's and 12 men's) will compete in **two medal events**:
- men's finals on Saturday, August 10 at 21:30
- women's finals on Sunday, August 11 at 15:30

Basketball was invented by James W. Naismith in the winter of 1891, when the 30-year-old physical education instructor from the International YMCA Training School in Springfield, Massachusetts came up with an indoor game that could be played between football and baseball seasons. Naismith wrote and developed the *basket ball*'s (initial two words) original thirteen rules and, through the YMCA network, quickly spread the news throughout the country. As the sport grew in popularity, Naismith neither sought publicity nor engaged in self-promotion. Although he never had the opportunity to witness basketball become the astonishing success it is today, Naismith's greatest joy occurred when he was sponsored by the National Association of Basketball Coaches to see the sport he created become an Olympic event at the 1936 Games held in Berlin, Germany.

Basketball first featured as a demonstration sport at the St. Louis 1904 Olympics. It was also played as an exhibition event at the 1924 Paris Games. In 1936, it became an official Olympic sport in Berlin and has been consistently featured since. Women's basketball made its debut 40 years later, at the Montreal Games in 1976. The United States stands as the most successful country in Olympic basketball, with the men's teams having secured victory in 16 out of 19 tournaments they participated in, including seven consecutive titles from 1936 through 1968. Similarly, the women's teams from the United States have claimed victory in eight out of the ten tournaments they competed in, enjoying a streak of seven consecutive wins from 1996 to 2020.

BASKETBALL 3X3

The 3×3 basketball events for the 2024 Paris Games will take place between July 30 and August 5 and will be played at *Place de la Concorde*.

In 3×3 basketball, teams of three players compete on a half-court, with both attacking and defending the same hoop depending on ball possession. The victor is determined by the highest score at the end of the 10-minute period or the first team to reach 21 points. Unlike conventional basketball, where the three-point line applies, in 3×3 basketball, shots made outside the line earn two points, while those inside it earn one point.

Despite the shorter duration of 3×3 games, these players need to demonstrate just as much flexibility, skill and anticipation as classic basketball players.

A total of 16 teams (8 women's and 8 men's) will compete in **two medal events**:
- women's finals on Monday, August 5 at 22:05
- men's finals on Monday, August 5 at 22:35

Considered to be the number one urban sport in the world, 3×3 basketball developed from a creative variation of basketball with a less formal structure – street basketball. Beginning in the late 2000s, 3×3 game rules started to become standardized throughout the United States, with events held across the country welcoming teams and players from all skill levels. The International Basketball Federation's endorsement of 3×3 events underscores the sport's surging popularity, characterized by its vibrant atmosphere, fueled by the presence of DJs and music, creating an electrifying experience for participants and spectators alike.

3×3 basketball made its worldwide competitive introduction at the Singapore 2010 *Youth* Olympic Games. Subsequently, world championships in both open and under 18 categories have become regular fixtures. Following its introduction at the Nanjing 2014 and Buenos Aires 2018 *Youth* Olympic Games, 3×3 basketball made its Olympic debut at the Tokyo 2020 Games, where the first titles were awarded. Latvia secured the gold medal in the men's competition, while the United States triumphed in the women's category.

BEACH VOLLEYBALL

The beach volleyball tournaments at the 2024 Olympics will take place from July 27 to August 10 at the Tour Eiffel Stadium in *Champ de Mars*.

Beach volleyball is played by two teams of two members each, on a sand court measuring 16 meters in length and 8 meters in width—slightly smaller than an indoor court—divided by a net. The net height is the same as indoor volleyball at 2.24 meters for women and 2.43 meters for men.

The Olympic beach volleyball competition comprises two stages for both women and men: preliminary rounds and playoffs or single elimination. During the preliminary rounds, the 24 teams are distributed into six pools of four teams each. The top two from each pool and four third-place teams advance to the single elimination round. The tournament continues in a single elimination format, with the round of 16, quarter-finals, and semi-finals, leading to the gold medal match between the semi-final winners and the bronze-medal match between the losing semi-finalists.

Each country is limited to two teams, with one spot reserved for the host nation and another for a randomly selected wild-card country. In the event that any Olympic region is not represented, the highest-ranked team from that continent qualifies for the tournament.

In beach volleyball, the first team to win two sets wins the match. The first two sets are played to 21 points each and the third set, if necessary, is played to 15 points. As there are only two members per team, players have a lot more ground to cover, which means they need lightning-fast reflexes. Matches are played outdoors, where wind, sun, and rain can affect playing conditions; athletes therefore need to be very versatile and adapt to the elements in order to succeed.

A total of 48 teams (24 women's and 24 men's) will compete in two medal events:
- women's finals on Friday, August 9 at 22:30
- men's finals on Saturday, August 10 at 22:30

A variation of volleyball played on sand first appeared on the beaches of Santa Monica, California in the 1920s. The first beach volleyball tournament took place in 1947 and the first circuit was launched in the 1950s, involving hundreds of players on Californian beaches. The first professional players' union was established in the 1980s and the inaugural international tournament was held in 1987.

Beach volleyball made its official Olympic debut at the Atlanta 1996 Games, after first appearing as a demonstration sport at the 1992 Games in Barcelona. The inaugural tournament featured 24 teams for men and 16 for women, expanding to 24 for both genders in Sydney 2000. Participating countries could enter two qualified teams, which proved particularly effective for two nations in 1996. The men's final was USA vs USA and the women's was Brazil vs Brazil. In fact, Brazil and the USA have achieved considerable success in the sport, collectively winning 24 Olympic medals (including 10 golds) out of a possible 42. The only other nations to clinch gold have been Germany in the men's (London 2012) and women's (Rio de Janeiro 2016) tournaments, Australia in the women's competition (Sydney 2000), and Norway in the men's event (Tokyo 2020).

BOXING

The boxing competitions at the 2024 Games are scheduled to run from July 27 to August 10. Preliminary matches will unfold at North Paris Arena in *Villepinte*, with the medal rounds (semifinals and finals) staged at the Roland Garros Stadium.

Male boxers will clash in seven weight classes, while female boxers will contest matches in six weight categories. The competition follows a straight elimination format from the beginning, with no box-off for third place. Instead, both losing semi-finalists are awarded bronze medals.

Olympic boxing operates under a distinct set of regulations. Prior to the 2012 London Games, exclusively amateur boxers participated, making the Olympics a launching pad for many renowned athletes, including the legendary Cassius Clay, later known as Muhammad Ali. However, since the Rio de Janeiro 2016 Games, professional boxers have been permitted to qualify as well.

Between 1984 and 2012, male boxers were required to wear protective headgear but the rule was abandoned starting with the 2016 Olympics. Female boxers are still obliged to wear head guards during their matches.

In each bout, three rounds of three minutes each are contested, with a one-minute break between them. At the conclusion of each round, judges evaluate the performance based on specific criteria and allocate ten points to the winner. The loser receives a score ranging from seven to nine points, reflecting their performance level. Following the conclusion of the bout, judges aggregate the round scores to determine the ultimate winner.

Boxers or pugilists need exceptional physical conditioning, including speed, strength, endurance, agility, and flexibility. Mastering boxing techniques such as footwork, punching, defense and counter-attacks is crucial. Fighters also need to be strategic thinkers, capable of analyzing their opponents' strengths and weaknesses, adjusting their tactics accordingly, and making split-second decisions in the ring. This includes understanding ring positioning, timing, distance management and effective use of feints and combinations.

The boxing program for Paris will feature **thirteen events** in total (seven for men and six for women):
- women's 60 kg finals on Tuesday, August 6 at 23:06
- men's 63.5 kg finals on Wednesday, August 7 at 22:34
- men's 80 kg finals on Wednesday, August 7 at 22:51
- men's 51 kg finals on Thursday, August 8 at 22:34
- women's 54 kg finals on Thursday, August 8 at 22:51
- men's 71 kg finals on Friday, August 9 at 21:30
- women's 50 kg finals on Friday, August 9 at 21:47
- men's 92 kg finals on Friday, August 9 at 22:34
- women's 66 kg finals on Friday, August 9 at 22:51
- women's 57 kg finals on Saturday, August 10 at 21:30
- men's 57 kg finals on Saturday, August 10 at 21:47
- women's 75 kg finals on Saturday, August 10 at 22:34
- men's +92 kg finals on Saturday, August 10 at 22:51

Humans have engaged in hand-to-hand combat since the earliest days of ancient history. The origins of boxing as a sport remain uncertain, but it has a rich history spanning several civilizations. The earliest visual evidence of boxing comes from Egypt and Sumer, both from the third millennium BC. These early Middle-Eastern and Egyptian depictions showed contests where fighters were either bare-fisted or had a band supporting the wrist. The earliest evidence of the use of gloves can be found in Minoan Crete around 1500–1400 BC. Various types of boxing also existed in ancient India.

Boxing became an established sport in ancient Greece, where it was included as an event in the 23rd Olympiad, as early as 688 BC. Known as *pygmachia*, Greek boxing was initially bare-handed, with fighters wearing leather straps around their hands for protection. There were no rounds and boxers fought until one of them acknowledged defeat or could not continue. Weight categories were not used, which meant heavier fighters had a tendency to dominate.

It continued to be popular in ancient Rome, where it was known as *pugilatus*. Fighters protected their knuckles with leather strips wrapped around their fists. Eventually harder leather was used and the strips became a weapon. Metal studs were introduced to the strips to make the *cestus*. Fighting events were held at Roman amphitheatres.

Boxing seemed to disappear with the fall of the Roman Empire, before resurfacing in the 17th century. It underwent substantial modernization in the 18th and 19th centuries, particularly in England. Rules were established, including the use of padded gloves, the introduction of weight classes, and regulations governing fouls and rounds.

The first officially sanctioned rules devised by John Chambers and endorsed by Marquess of Queensberry in 1867, laid the foundation for modern boxing. These rules also outlined the size and shape of the boxing ring, as well as how long the rounds should be and how much downtime each fighter gets. While there were still plenty of fights going on that didn't follow the Queensberry Rules, they marked an important period in boxing history shaping the sport as we recognize it today.

Boxing debuted as a men's event at the 1904 Summer Olympics in St. Louis, initially featuring only North American boxers due to limited participation. Since the 1908 Games, boxing has been contested at every Summer Olympics, except for the 1912 Games in Stockholm, because Swedish law banned the sport at the time.

Women's boxing was introduced to the Olympic program for the first time, at the London 2012 Games. As of 2016, professional fighters are allowed to compete in Olympic events previously being limited to amateur or state-funded boxers.

USA athletes have achieved the most Olympic success in boxing, winning 117 medals. Cuba and Great Britain have also demonstrated notable performances in the sport, with Cuban athletes securing 78 and British competitors earning 62 medals.

Numerous boxers have transitioned to professional careers after winning Olympic titles. Cassius Clay, later known as Muhammad Ali (1960 Rome), Sugar Ray Leonard (1976 Montreal), Vladimir Klitschko (1996 Atlanta), Oleksandr Usyk and Anthony Joshua (both in 2012 London) went on to achieve further success in the professional arena, securing world titles.

BREAKING

Breaking will be making its Olympic debut as a sport at the 2024 Games.

The events will feature breakdancers engaging in captivating face-to-face battles. Athletes will showcase a combination of power moves, including windmills, the six-step and freezes, while adapting and improvising to the DJ's tracks. Their goal is to impress the judges and earn high scores to claim the inaugural Olympic breaking title.

A total of 32 competitors (16 B-Girls and 16 B-Boys) will contest in *Place de la Concorde* across **two medal events:**
- women's finals on Friday, August 9 at 21:23
- men's finals on Saturday, August 10 at 21:23

Breaking also known as breakdancing, is a style of dance that originated in the United States in the 1970s. It is closely associated with the rise of hip-hop culture, where DJs created rhythmic breaks specifically for dancers. This art form took shape at the lively block parties in the Bronx, becoming an integral part of hip-hop culture. Breaking is characterized by its acrobatic movements, stylized footwork and the key roles played by the DJ and the MC during battles.

Breakdancing consists mainly of four kinds of movement — toprock, downrock, power moves and freezes — and is typically set to songs containing drum breaks, especially in funk, soul, and hip-hop.

International competitions began in the 1990s, spreading across the globe and popularizing the dance form within hip-hop communities and among the general public.

Breaking was featured at the Summer *Youth* Olympic Games in Buenos Aires in 2018. Its remarkable success at the Games in Argentina led to its inclusion in the Paris 2024 Olympic program as a new sport.

CANOE SLALOM AND SPRINT

Canoeing competitions at the 2024 Olympics are scheduled to run across two main disciplines: canoe slalom events are set to run from July 27 to August 5, while canoe sprint races are scheduled between August 6 and 10. Both canoe slalom and sprint events will be staged at the National Olympic Nautical Stadium of Île-de-France in *Vaires-sur-Marne*.

The canoe-kayak events include two different disciplines that are both part of the Olympic program: canoe-kayak sprint and canoe-kayak slalom. Both involve different types of boats: canoes and kayaks. Canoes have an open hull with high sides, while kayaks have a closed cockpit with a small opening for the paddler's legs. In kayaking, participants are seated and use a double-bladed paddle, whereas canoeists kneel in their boats and use a single-blade paddle.

Canoe-kayak sprint events are held at *flatwater* venues, similar to rowing events. In races, competitors follow a straight line with eight lanes, aiming to reach the finish line before their opponents. Distances covered in these races include 200, 500, and 1000 meters. There are Olympic events for individual athletes (canoe single – C-1 and kayak single – K-1), pairs (canoe double – C-2 and kayak double – K-2), and crews of four people (kayak four – K-4).

Canoe-kayak slalom competitions are timed races held on a *whitewater* course, featuring up to twenty-five gates that participants must navigate through. Each gate must be passed in a specific sequence. Touching a gate incurs a two-second penalty, while missing a gate results in a hefty fifty-second penalty, considerably impacting the athlete's overall race time. This penalty system underscores the importance of precision and accuracy in navigating the course, as avoiding penalties is crucial for achieving a good result in the competition.

Similar to previous editions, the upcoming competition will include sixteen events, though with some adjustments to the program lineup. The men's C-2 and K-2 1000 meters events will be replaced with half of their distance, namely the men's C-2 and K-2 500 meters, aligning with the women's program. Paris 2024 will also introduce the men's and women's slalom kayak cross events, replacing the men's and women's K-1 200-meter sprint races.

In the kayak cross events for both men and women, four athletes will simultaneously begin from a start ramp, navigating a course marked with ten gates or obstacles that require maneuvers such as kayak rails. The first two athletes to cross the finish line without missing any gates will advance to the next round.

In canoe slalom, athletes must possess a mix of agility, balance, strength, and endurance to navigate the demanding whitewater course. On the other hand, in canoe sprint, competitors depend predominantly on explosive power and speed to propel their boats across flatwater courses.

Canoe slalom competitions will feature **six events**:
- women's K-1 kayak single finals on Sunday, July 28 at 17:45
- men's C-1 canoe single finals on Monday, July 29 at 17:20
- women's C-1 canoe single finals on Wednesday, July 31 at 17:25
- men's K-1 kayak single finals on Thursday, August 1 at 17:30
- women's KX-1 kayak cross finals on Monday, August 5 at 16:55
- men's KX-1 kayak cross finals on Monday, August 5 at 17:00

Canoe sprint races will consist of **ten events**:
- men's C-2 canoe double 500 m finals on Thursday, August 8 at 13:30
- women's K-4 kayak four 500 m finals on Thursday, August 8 at 13:40
- men's K-4 kayak four 500 m finals on Thursday, August 8 at 13:50
- women's C-2 canoe double 500 m finals on Friday, August 9 at 12:50
- women's K-2 kayak double 500 m finals on Friday, August 9 at 13:10
- men's K-2 kayak double 500 m finals on Friday, August 9 at 13:30
- men's C-1 canoe single 1000 m finals on Friday, August 9 at 13:50
- women's K-1 kayak single 500 m finals on Saturday, August 10 at 13:00
- men's K-1 kayak single 1000 m finals on Saturday, August 10 at 13:20
- women's C-1 canoe single 200 m finals on Saturday, August 10 at 13:50

It is believed that kayaks originated in Greenland and were primarily used by Eskimos for hunting, fishing, and transportation. Conversely, canoes were used for transport and trade across various regions worldwide. Competitions in canoe-kayak sports began to emerge in the mid-19th century.

Established in 1866, the London Royal Canoe Club was the first organization dedicated to the development of the sport. By the 1890s, canoeing and kayaking had gained significant popularity across Europe. The increasing interest during the early 1900s prompted the need for international structure. In 1924, the predecessor of the International Canoe Federation, the *Internationale Repräsentantenschaft Kanusport*, was formed by German, Austrian, and Swedish delegates.

Canoe sprint was officially introduced as an Olympic sport at the 1936 Games in Berlin, after it had already featured as a demonstration event at the 1924 Olympics. Women's participation started in 1948 at the London Games, initially limited to one discipline, contrasting with the eight disciplines available to men. Though there was only one event, K-1 500 meters, it marked an important step for women in the development of this sport. Races now are predominantly 500 or 1000 meters long, although men's 10-kilometer events were also included from 1936 to 1956.

Canoe slalom made its Olympic debut at the 1972 Games in Munich, introducing K-1, C-1 and C-2 classes for men, along with C-1 for women. Despite its success, the costs for building a whitewater course were considered too high and the discipline disappeared from the Olympic program for two decades. Canoe slalom made a return at the 1992 Barcelona Games, becoming a permanent fixture on the Olympic canoe and kayaking program.

Historically, athletes from European nations have enjoyed significant success at the Games. Germany has secured a total of 77 Olympic medals, including an impressive 34 golds. Similarly, Hungary has amassed a remarkable tally of 86 Olympic medals, with 28 of them being gold.

CYCLING BMX FREESTYLE

The BMX freestyle events in Paris are scheduled for July 30 and 31 at *Place de la Concorde*.

Freestyle BMX, characterized by stunt riding on BMX bikes, is an extreme sport rooted in BMX racing, comprising five disciplines: street, park, vert, trails and flatland. The BMX freestyle park event is included in the Olympic program.

Taking place in an urban park setting, the BMX freestyle competitions challenge riders to execute as many tricks as possible within 60 seconds. The scores are based on the difficulty of the tricks, the height of their jumps, as well as the creativity and style of the routine.

The competitors in BMX freestyle park are known for their athleticism, creativity, and daring feats. They often come from diverse backgrounds in BMX riding and dedicate years to refining their skills to compete at the highest level.

A total of 24 riders (12 women and 12 men) will compete for **two medal events**:
- women's finals on Wednesday, July 31 at 13:10
- men's finals on Wednesday, July 31 at 14:45

Emerging from the racing culture that originated in California during the 1970s, BMX freestyle was born out of the imagination of children and teenagers in the region inspired by the moves of riders and keen to imitate their heroes. The sport became increasingly popular over subsequent decades and integrated the programs of extreme sports competitions. The inaugural BMX Freestyle World Cup was organized in 2016.

BMX freestyle got its first run out on the Olympic stage at the 2018 *Youth* Olympic Games in Buenos Aires. Delivering an electrifying spectacle before packed crowds, its captivating performances earned it a spot in the Olympic program for the first time at the 2020 Games in Tokyo, eventually held in 2021. Charlotte Worthington of Great Britain and Logan Martin of Australia emerged as the first Olympic champions in the women's and men's categories, respectively.

CYCLING BMX RACING

The BMX race events in 2024 will take place on August 1 and 2 on the BMX stadium next to the Vélodrome National de Saint-Quentin-en-Yvelines in *Montigny-le-Bretonneux*, a south-western suburb of Paris.

BMX racing is a type of off-road bicycle racing, characterized by its explosive nature, contrasting with the more traditional cycling disciplines. Its format was derived from motocross racing.

In BMX Racing, participants require an intense burst of energy over a brief period lasting a few seconds. Races unfold as single-lap sprints on purpose-built off-road tracks. These tracks feature starting gates for up to eight racers, a groomed, serpentine, dirt race course made of various jumps and rollers, culminating with the finish line, where speed and quick reactions determine the winner.

The track, approximately 15 feet (4.6 meters) wide, has large banked corners, which are angled inward, facilitating speed maintenance for riders. Launching from a gate atop an 8-meter-high start hill, competitors navigate the 400-meter track, reaching speeds of up to 60 km/h. Quick reactions and explosive power are essential to burst out of the gates in front of the pack, seizing an early lead and maintaining it until the finish line. The final race is often a thrilling spectacle, captivating viewers as they watch with eager anticipation.

A total of 48 riders (24 women and 24 men) will compete for **two medal events**:
- men's finals on Friday, August 2 at 21:35
- women's finals on Friday, August 2 at 21:50

BMX racing emerged from the motocross craze that surged in California during the 1960s. Although informal bicycle racing existed to varying degrees, it was in Southern California where BMX started to become organized and resemble the modern sport. The first race took place on 1969.

Children had fun imitating their idols on their bikes and BMX began developing into a proper sport in the early 1980s. The first BMX world championships were held in 1982.

BMX racing made its debut as a medal sport at the 2008 Olympics in Beijing, with Anne-Caroline Chausson of France emerging as the women's champion and Māris Štrombergs of Latvia claiming victory in the men's category, thereby becoming the first Olympic champions in the discipline.

CYCLING MOUNTAIN BIKE

Mountain bike racing is a competitive cycling sport that takes place on off-road terrain. It encompasses various events, with cross-country being the most common and the only one featured in the Olympics. In cross-country, riders complete multiple laps around a circuit or travel from point to point.

In the high-speed downhill event, participants descend a mountain slope, negotiating jumps and turns at high speeds. The four-cross event, which pits four riders against each other on a demanding course, is popular among spectators. Other competitions include the team relay and, previously, the dual slalom.

The cross-country Olympic race features a mass start and participants contest multiple laps around a loop on mountainous, rough terrain. They test their technique, as they face near-vertical climbs and challenge their descending skills on the way back down. Riders also require endurance and stamina as it can take 1h20 to 1h40 to complete an intense course full of twists and turns, covering tens of kilometers during the event.

Mountain bikes are easily distinguished from standard racing bikes by several prominent features. Key differences include their thicker, knobby tires, providing more off-road grip and their straight or flat handlebars, making it easier to climb. Additionally, many mountain bikes feature suspension systems in their forks in order to make riding on bumpy terrain more comfortable.

It's worth noting that not all mountain bikes are identical; those utilized for downhill competitions differ from those used for cross-country riding. There are very few regulations specific to them, as one of the only exceptions is the prohibition of spiked tires.

A total of 72 riders (36 women and 36 men) will compete on Élancourt Hill for **two medal events**:
- women's finals on Sunday, July 28 at 14:10
- men's finals on Monday, July 29 at 14:10

Off-road cycling has existed for a long time, mostly in the form of cyclo-cross, although it has never been part of the Olympic program. In the early 1970s, enthusiasts across the United States started modifying bicycles for off-road use. In the 1990s, the first mountain bikes that could withstand impacts experienced during riding were developed. At first mostly a recreational activity, mountain biking also evolved into a competitive sport and quickly became popular not only in the United States, but also in the traditional cycling nations of Europe. The first informal competitions took place in the 1980s before the inaugural official world championships were held in the 1990s.

In 1996, cross-country mountain biking events, featuring individual races for both women and men, were introduced to the Olympic Games, marking their inclusion exactly a century after the debut of road and track cycling events.

Throughout its brief Olympic history, French and Swiss athletes have regularly finished on the podium in this event, earning a total of 16 out of the 42 medals awarded. France has secured six medals, four of them gold, while Switzerland has won ten medals, including two golds.

CYCLING ROAD

Road cycling occurs outdoors primarily on paved roads. Road racing stands as the most popular professional form of bicycle racing, in terms of numbers of competitors, events and spectators. The two most common competition formats are: mass start events, where riders start simultaneously and race towards a designated finish line; and time trials, where individual riders or teams race a course alone against the clock. Stage races or "tours" take multiple days, and consist of several mass-start or time-trial stages ridden consecutively. The pinnacle of road cycling is the Tour de France, a three-week stage race that can attract over 500,000 roadside supporters a day.

At the Olympic Games, road cycling comprises two distinct events: the road race and the individual time trial.

The road race, where all riders set off at the same time in a mass start, is highly a tactical feat of endurance. Often, the race is won in a sprint finish over the last few hundred meters, which means riders need to position themselves perfectly and conserve their energy in the first part of the race. In 2024, competitors will compete in and around Paris (Pont d'Iéna–Trocadéro), covering 158 kilometers in the women's event and 273 kilometers in the men's.

The time trial is a solo effort in which the riders set off at intermittent times rather than in a grouped peloton. It involves a significantly shorter distance compared to the road race. Success in this discipline demands consistency, concentration and the ability to maintain effective aerodynamic positioning and power output. In 2024, both races will feature a 32.4-kilometer course in and around Paris (Pont Alexandre III).

Paris 2024's road cycling consists in **four medal events**:
- women's time trial finals on Saturday, July 27 at 14:30
- men's time trial finals on Saturday, July 27 at 16:34
- men's road race finals on Saturday, August 3 at 11:00
- women's road race finals on Sunday, August 4 at 14:00

Cycling is composed of a variety of disciplines, reflecting both its age-old past and its modern outlook, with road cycling being the earliest form of the sport. In the 19th century, cycling enjoyed a surge in popularity, becoming a leisure pastime with the invention of the bicycle. Organized races soon followed, with documented records tracing back to 1868 at the Parc de Saint Cloud in Paris. Professional racing originated in Western Europe, particularly in France, Spain, Italy, and Belgium where the prestigious Liège–Bastogne–Liège race, established in 1892, continues to run every year.

Road cycling is one of the longest standing Olympic events, as it featured in the sporting program at the first modern Olympiad in 1896 in Athens. Left out of three editions between 1900 and 1908, road cycling has returned to 1912 Stockholm Games where the men's individual time trial was introduced. The women's road race was added to the Olympic program in the 1984 Los Angeles Games, while the women's time trial made its debut in 1996.

Prior to 1996, professional riders were not allowed to participate in the Olympic Games. However, since the Atlanta Games of that year, members of the professional cycling world have been permitted to compete, enhancing the prestige of Olympic events and attracting the world's most renowned cyclists.

CYCLING TRACK

Track cycling is held within a velodrome, a bowl-shaped arena measuring 250 meters (273.4 yards), featuring various race formats for individuals and teams. Cyclists navigate the track with impressive ease. At the 2024 Olympics Vélodrome National de Saint-Quentin-en-Yvelines will host the track cycling events.

Unlike road bicycles, track bicycles are fixed-gear and don't have brakes. Different types of races occur on the track, each with their own specific rules and techniques. Some rely more heavily on tactics, while others prioritize strength and power. Therefore, the effort needed to complete a lap in the individual sprint is quite different from that required in the 25-kilometer group omnium race.

At the Olympic Games, there are six track cycling events: sprint, team sprint, keirin, team pursuit, omnium, and madison. All six events are held for both women and men.

Sprint

The sprint or match sprint is a race between two riders over three laps of the track. Unlike the team sprint, competitors don't launch into full speed from the starting signal. Although the goal is simple, get to the line ahead of your opponent, there are serious amounts of tactics involved. Men's sprint has been an Olympic event at every Games except 1904, which featured races at various distances and 1912, which had no track cycling events. Women's sprints have been contested at every Olympics since 1988.

Team Sprint

In the team sprint, two teams of three riders race against each other, starting on opposite sides of the track. Despite its name, it is not a conventional cycling sprint event – it is rather a team time trial held over three laps of velodrome. Cyclists accelerate up to top speeds, with each athlete completing one lap of the track before the final sprint to the finish. The overall time of the last rider determines the winning team. The team sprint has been an Olympic event for men since 2000 and for women since 2012.

Keirin

The last of the sprint events is the keirin. Originating from Japan around 1948 for gambling purposes and literally translating to "racing cycle" in Japanese, keirin Olympic races cover a distance of 1.5 kilometers (0.93 miles), equivalent to six velodrome laps. During the keirin cycling race, six riders follow a pacing motorbike for the initial three laps. It sets off at 30 km/h (19 mph) and gradually increases its speed to 50 (31 mph) for men and from 25 (16 mph) to 45 km/h (28 mph) for women by the final lap. Riders must stay behind the motorbike and cannot pass it until it exits the track with three laps to go. Once it leaves, cyclists sprint for victory, with the first rider to cross emerging victorious. Winning speeds can exceed 70 km/h (43 mph). Keirin became an official Olympic event in 2000 for men and in 2012 for women.

Team Pursuit

In the team pursuit, squads of four both men and women compete over a four-kilometer distance, with their opponents positioned on the other side of the track. Cyclists maintain a tight formation, taking turns leading the group. After completing their stint at the front, the lead rider moves aside, swings up the track and rejoins the team at the back. Timing is based on the third member of the squad to cross the finish line, although the race may conclude if one team catches up with the other. The men's event debuted at the Olympics in 1908, while women began competing in 2012.

Omnium

The Omnium is a competition based on points, consisting of four distinct races where all riders start together. The four bunch races are: Scratch Race, Tempo Race, Elimination Race, and Points Race.

The Omnium starts off with a basic Scratch Race, covering 10 kilometers for men and 7.5 kilometers for women, with the first rider across the finish line declared the winner. Following this is the Tempo Race, with the same distances, where riders sprint for points every lap after the first four laps. Riders who lap the field earn 20 points, while those who are dropped and lapped lose 20 points. The third is the Elimination Race, featuring sprints every two laps, with the last rider across the line eliminated; the process continues until just one competitor remains. The final event is the Points Race, spanning 25 kilometers for men and 20 kilometers for women. Points are granted every ten laps to the top four riders (5, 3, 2, and 1 point), with double points awarded for the final sprint. Gaining a lap on the field earns a rider 20 points, whereas being lapped results in a 20-point penalty. After completing all four events, the accumulated points determine the medalists, with the cyclist gathering the highest total points crowned the winner. The Omnium made its Olympic debut for both men and women in 2012.

Madison

The Madison is a relay race involving two riders, with only one actively participating at any given time. During the race, points are awarded through intermediate sprints. Additionally, teams can accumulate points by lapping the field, yet they lose points if they get lapped. The final sprint offers double points, with the team that has the highest point tally being declared the winner.

In the men's race, spanning 200 laps (50 kilometers), and the women's race, covering 120 laps (30 kilometers), fifteen teams navigate the velodrome. Each rider takes turns being "active" on the track while the "inactive" rider coasts at a slower pace on the upper bank of the track until they swap positions. Typically, this exciting sling-shot movement is created by teammates gripping hands and then catapulting one another forward into action. This exchange can occur anywhere on the track and as frequently as desired. Named after Madison Square Garden in New York City, where it was first held, the event is referred to as "l'américaine" in French. Initially featured in the men's Olympic event from 2000 to 2008, it was absent from the 2012 and 2016 Games but reinstated in 2020. Notably, 2020 marked the debut of the women's Madison event in Olympic history.

The track cycling races in Paris will consist of **twelve medal events**:
- women's team sprint finals on Monday, August 5 at 19:58
- men's team sprint finals on Tuesday, August 6 at 20:07
- men's team pursuit finals on Wednesday, August 7 at 18:33
- women's team pursuit finals on Wednesday, August 7 at 18:57
- women's keirin finals on Thursday, August 8 at 19:11
- men's omnium finals on Thursday, August 8 at 19:27
- women's madison finals on Friday, August 9 at 18:09
- men's sprint finals on Friday, August 9 at 19:38
- men's madison finals on Saturday, August 10 at 17:59
- men's keirin finals on Sunday, August 11 at 13:32
- women's sprint finals on Sunday, August 11 at 13:44
- women's omnium finals on Sunday, August 11 at 13:56

The first bicycles were invented in the 1850s, particularly in France, and looked quite different to the bikes we know today. But it wasn't until the 1870s that England developed competitive cycling events on wooden indoor tracks, with the first six-day race held in London in 1878. One of the key attractions of indoor track racing was its ability to manage spectators effectively, allowing organizers to charge entrance fees, thus making track cycling a profitable sport. These early races attracted crowds of up to 2,000 people. Additionally, indoor tracks facilitated year-round cycling for the first time. The main early centers for track racing in Great Britain were Birmingham, Sheffield, Liverpool, Manchester, and London. Track cycling quickly grew in popularity and continued to develop with the creation of the International Cycling Association. This enabled the organization of the first world championships in Chicago in 1893.

Over the span of more then a century, track cycling has witnessed notable transformations, particularly concerning the bikes themselves, which have been engineered to be lighter and more aerodynamic, enabling athletes to achieve increasingly faster times. Furthermore, track lengths have undergone gradual reductions. Initially, velodromes varied in length from 130 to 500 meters. From the 1960s to 1989, a standardized length of 333.333 meters was commonly used for international competitions. Since 1990, international velodromes have adopted a standardized length of 250 meters (273.403 yd).

A long-standing Olympic discipline, track cycling has been featured in every modern Olympics except the 1912 Games in Stockholm. Women had to wait until the 1988 Games in Seoul to join the program. The sport was moved indoors since 2000 Olympics in Sydney, Australia, mainly because of the hot weather.

Over the course of its more than 120-year history, European nations have consistently dominated the medal standings in the track cycling events. Notably the UK, boasting 79 medals, including 33 golds, and France, with 67 medals, including 28 golds.

During the inaugural modern Summer Olympic Games in 1896, Athens hosted five men's cycling track events, featuring nineteen cyclists from five nations.

The first event, the 100-kilometer race, occurred on April 8th, where cyclists had to complete 300 circuits of the track. Léon Flameng of France emerged victorious in this race.

April 11th saw three events, all remarkably won by Paul Masson of France. The sprint, covering a distance of 2 kilometers or six laps, was followed by the 10 kilometers race, consisting of 30 laps. This marked the only instance where the 10-kilometer track race was part of the Olympic cycling program. The time trial, the third event scheduled that day, featured a unique distance of one-third of a kilometer, a format not repeated until 1928 when it became one kilometer.

Concluding the cycling track events on April 13th was the 12-hour race, claimed by Adolf Schmal of Austria. This race marked the final event of the 1896 Summer Olympic Games.

DIVING

The diving competitions at the 2024 Summer Games will be held from July 27 to August 10 at the Aquatics Center in Paris.

Diving is contested from the 3-meter springboard and the 10-meter platform. The 3-meter springboard enables divers to leap even higher into the air, while the high dive is performed from fixed platform positioned 10 meters above the water. The individual and synchronized competitions take place at both heights.

Dives receive scores based on various criteria, such as the aesthetic appeal of the diver's movements, the complexity of the dive, and the quality of the diver's entry into the water. Synchronized diving is also judged by how well the two divers can match each other's movements.

136 divers will compete across **eight medal events**:
- women's 3 m synchronized springboard finals on Saturday, July 27 at 11:00
- men's 10 m synchronized platform finals on Monday, July 29 at 11:00
- women's 10 m synchronized platform finals on Wednesday, July 31 at 11:00
- men's 3 m synchronized springboard finals on Friday, August 2 at 11:00
- women's 10 m platform finals on Tuesday, August 6 at 15:00
- men's 3 m springboard finals on Thursday, August 8 at 15:00
- women's 3 m springboard finals on Friday, August 9 at 15:00
- men's 10 m platform finals on Saturday, August 10 at 15:00

In the 19th century, diving first became popular in Sweden and Germany, influenced by gymnasts who showcased their acrobatic skills by diving into water, emphasizing a blend of athleticism and grace. In the late 19th century, Swedish divers journeyed to Great Britain to present their abilities through demonstrations. This led to the sport gaining popularity in England, with the first world championship event held there in 1895. The event consisted of standing and running dives from either 15 or 30 feet (4.6 or 9.1 meters).

Diving was quick to integrate the Olympic sport program, making its debut in the 1904 St. Louis Games. Women's events were contested for the first time at the 1912 Stockholm Games. Since the 1928 Olympics onward, the diving competitions have remained unchanged until 1996, featuring 2 women's and 2 men's events. Four years later in Sydney, the addition of synchronized diving for both the springboard and platform events expanded the lineup to eight events (4 women's and 4 men's events).

Initially, USA athletes dominated diving events at the Games, but in recent Olympics, Chinese competitors have proven formidable. At the Tokyo 2020 Games, Chinese athletes claimed 12 out of 24 available diving medals, including seven golds.

EQUESTRIAN

The Equestrian competitions in 2024 will take place between July 27 and August 6 at the Château de Versailles.

The events held at the Olympic Games are jumping, dressage, and eventing. In each of these disciplines, medals are given out for both individual and team performances. All events are open, meaning that both men and women compete on equal terms.

In the jumping discipline, riders and horses are timed as they jump over obstacles, knocking over as few as possible – with penalties for each obstacle toppled. Agility, technique and harmony between the horse and rider are essential.

Dressage represents the pinnacle of horse training, where horse and rider execute intricate movements choreographed to music. Judges assess the grace and fluency of their performance.

Eventing combines jumping and dressage with cross-country – a challenging test of endurance and experience over a long course combining solid and natural obstacles. The horse and rider with the most versatile skills across all three disciplines win this combined event.

The equestrian disciplines in Paris will comprise **six medal events**:
- team eventing finals on Monday, July 29 at 12:15
- individual eventing finals on Monday, July 29 at 15:00
- team jumping finals on Friday, August 2 at 14:00
- team dressage finals on Saturday, August 3 at 10:00
- individual dressage finals on Sunday, August 4 at 10:00
- individual jumping finals on Tuesday, August 6 at 10:00

Equestrian events originated in ancient Greece, where it was thought that a perfect partnership was needed if rider and horse were to survive in battle. To prepare horses for warfare, the Greeks pioneered dressage as a method of training. Equestrian events appeared at the ancient Olympic Games in the form of chariot racing, which was a daring and exciting spectacle.

Equestrian competitions were first held at the 1900 Paris Olympic Games, although individual jumping was the only one that resembled any of the disciplines seen today. The other three events were high jump, long jump, and mail coach. The equestrian sports weren't held in 1904 and 1908 despite the development of the current three disciplines, as the Olympic host couldn't stage this kind of event. They returned in 1912 in Stockholm, where the now regular disciplines of dressage, eventing, and jumping were included.

Up until 1948 participation in the Olympics was exclusive to military officers. The restriction was lifted in the Helsinki Games of 1952, permitting both civilians and women to contend for the medals.

Although women began participating in the dressage event for the first time in 1952, it wasn't until 1964 Games in Tokyo, that they gained access to all events. This makes equestrian the only entirely mixed sport at the Olympic Games.

FENCING

Fencing is a combat sport that features sword fighting. Two competitors, each wielding a weapon in one hand, face each other with the aim of landing strikes on valid target areas of the body to score points. Modern fencing comprises three disciplines: the foil, épée, and sabre, each with its own set of rules corresponding to the specific type of weapon utilized.

The sabre can weigh up to 500 grams and serves as both a cutting and thrusting weapon. Hits made with the point (tip), edge, or back of the blade are counted as valid in sabre, with the target area including the entire torso above the waist, as well as the head and arms.

In épée and foil, fencers only score when they strike their opponent with the point (tip) of their weapon.

Both the foil and the épée are intended as thrusting weapons, with the foil being restricted to a maximum weight of 500 grams and the épée allowed to weigh up to 775 grams. In épée the target area covers the entire body, from the mask down to the feet, while in foil the target area is the trunk only (torso, shoulders, and neck).

All three disciplines take place on a piste, which measures 14 meters in length and is 1.5 to 2 meters wide. Retreating off the end of the piste results in a point awarded to the opponent.

In individual matches, the first fencer to accumulate 15 points wins, or the fencer with the highest score after three periods, each lasting three minutes, with one-minute breaks between them. The clock halts between exchanges, with fencers returning to the *en garde* position to start again.

In team fencing, the winning team is either the first to score a total of 45 points or the team with the highest score when the allocated time expires.

The majority of competitive fencers tend to specialize in a particular discipline. Based on sword fighting, fencing requires speed, anticipation, reflexes and great mental strength. Quick footwork and a strong sense of balance are crucial, supporting both offensive and defensive maneuvers. Precision in executing attacks and parries, combined with impeccable timing, is also crucial for fencing.

A total of 212 fencers, with an equal distribution between men and women, will compete in Paris at the Grand Palais strip across **twelve medal events**:
- women's épée individual finals on Saturday, July 27 at 21:30
- men's sabre individual finals on Saturday, July 27 at 21:55
- women's foil individual finals on Sunday, July 28 at 21:45
- men's épée individual finals on Sunday, July 28 at 22:15
- women's sabre individual finals on Monday, July 29 at 21:45
- men's foil individual finals on Monday, July 29 at 22:10
- women's épée team finals on Tuesday, July 30 at 20:30
- men's sabre team finals on Wednesday, July 31 at 20:30
- women's foil team finals on Thursday, August 1 at 20:30
- men's épée team finals on Friday, August 2 at 20:30
- women's sabre team finals on Saturday, August 3 at 20:00
- men's foil team finals on Sunday, August 4 at 20:30

Fencing's origins can be found in swordplay, which has been practiced for thousands of years – as evidenced by depictions of fencers dating from around 1190 BC in Egypt. Throughout history, swordsmanship was not only a pastime, but also a crucial skill for single combat and warfare, practiced widely by the ancient Persians, Babylonians, Greeks, and Romans, as well as by the Germanic tribes. Fencing, initially conceived as a method of military training, became a sport under the impulse of fencing masters from France, Italy, and Germany.

The significance of the modern sport grew towards the end of the 19th century, building upon the traditional skill set of swordsmanship. The Italian school altered the historical European martial art of classical fencing, and the French school refined that system. Today, fencing enjoys global popularity, with enthusiasts and competitors all over the world, generating fierce competition not only in Europe, but also Asia, Oceania, the Americas, and Africa.

Fencing is a long-standing Olympic sport, starting at the 1896 Games in Athens. It has been featured in every modern Summer Olympics along with track and field or athletics, cycling, swimming, and gymnastics.

The sabre is the only weapon consistently featured in every Games, starting in 1896. The épée was introduced at the Paris 1900 Olympics. The foil, which had already debuted in 1896, was held only as a display event in the 1908 Games, and thus no medals were awarded. In the 1904 Games, a fourth discipline of fencing known as singlestick was featured. It was dropped after that year and is not a part of modern fencing. Six events, men's team and individual for each of the three disciplines, sabre, foil, and épée, were contested for the first time at Antwerp 1920 Games.

Women's fencing made its Olympic debut in 1924 in Paris with the individual foil event. The women's team foil was added at the Rome 1960 Games. For several decades, foil remained the sole women's fencing event until the Atlanta 1996 Olympics, when both individual and team épée disciplines were introduced. The first women's individual sabre Olympic competition took place at the Athens 2004 Games, while women's team sabre was introduced for the first time in Beijing 2008.

In the medal standings, Italy leads with 130 medals (49 gold, 46 silver, and 35 bronze), followed closely by France, with 123 medals (44 gold, 43 silver, and 36 bronze), and Hungary with 90 medals (38 gold, 24 silver, and 28 bronze).

The most decorated fencer in Olympic history is Italy's Edoardo Mangiarotti who won thirteen medals, six golds, five silver and two bronze, across five Games despite his career being interrupted by World War II. Compatriot Nedo Nadi, has a historic and unequaled record: is the only fencer to have won a medal in every weapon category in a single edition of the Games. He won five gold medals in Antwerp in 1920: in the individual foil and sabre events, and in the team foil, épée and sabre events.

But the record of seven golds is held by Hungary's Aladar Gerevich, who remains the only athlete to win the same event, men's team sabre, at six consecutive Olympic Games from Los Angeles 1932 to Rome 1960. This incredible streak includes the cancellation of the 1940 and 1944 Games due to World War II, with Gerevich clinching his final gold at the age of 50. He won the individual sabre title at the London 1948 Games for a total haul of seven golds. Gerevich also earned one silver and two bronze medals throughout his remarkable Olympic career.

FIELD HOCKEY

The 2024 field hockey tournaments will take place between July 27 and August 9 at Stade Yves-du-Manoir, a legacy venue of the 1924 Paris Summer Olympics.

A field hockey match lasts for 60 minutes, divided into four periods of 15 minutes each. Each team comprises eleven players, including forwards, midfielders, defenders, and a goalkeeper. Touching the ball with hands or feet (except for goalkeepers) is prohibited. Teams have the option to make substitutions freely and frequently throughout the game, including playing without a goalkeeper temporarily if needed. The objective is to score more goals than the opponent. While group matches can end with a draw, shootout sessions are used in knockout games if necessary.

A hockey pitch measures 91.40 meters in length and 55 meters in width, featuring goals at each end surrounded by a D-shaped shooting area. Goals can only be scored from inside the opponent's shooting area. Players utilize hook-shaped sticks to drive, control and hit a hard ball, with only the flat side of the stick permitted for use. A fault can lead the referee to inflict a green card (2 minutes of suspension), yellow (5 minutes of suspension) or red (exclusion) for the offending player.

In its early days, field hockey was played on natural grass, which often made the game slower. The decision to move to synthetic turf intended to modernize the game, making it quicker. The pitch is also watered; this means the ball travels at an even faster pace.

Speed, technical skills and fun are the main characteristics of field hockey, an exciting and dynamic sport that requires endurance and great coordination.

A total of 24 teams (12 women's and 12 men's) will compete for **two medal events**:
- men's finals on Thursday, August 8 at 19:00
- women's finals on Friday, August 9 at 20:00

Although the word hockey itself has no clear origin, the common theory is that it takes its name from the French word *hocquet* meaning a shepherd's crook, in reference to the curved shape of a hockey stick. The sport has ancient roots, tracing back to antiquity. Historical evidence suggests that early forms or variations were played in Egypt and Persia (2000 BC) and Ethiopia (1000 BC). Records from museums indicate that hockey-like games were later played by the Romans and Greeks, as well as the Aztecs several centuries before Christopher Columbus's arrival in the New World. The modern game developed with the growing number of schools in 19th century England. Field hockey is now played globally, particularly in parts of Western Europe, South Asia, Southern Africa, Australia, New Zealand, Argentina, and parts of the United States, primarily New England and the mid-Atlantic states.

Field hockey debuted at the 1908 Games in London and became a permanent fixture in the Olympic program from 1928 Amsterdam Games. The women's competition joined the Olympic lineup at the 1980 Moscow Games. The Netherlands stands out as the top-performing nation in overall medal count, boasting 18 medals (6 gold, 6 silver and 6 bronze). The Dutch team also dominates the women's field hockey event, clinching 9 medals (4 gold, 2 silver and 3 bronze). India holds the record for the most gold medals, with 8 victories, all won in men's competition. From 1928 to 1964, India secured gold in seven out of eight Olympics. They claimed their most recent gold medal in the 1980 Games.

GOLF

The golf tournaments at the 2024 Games in Paris are scheduled to run from August 1 to 10 at Le Golf National in Guyancourt.

Golf is a club-and-ball sport in which players use different clubs to strike a ball into a sequence of holes on a course, aiming to complete each hole in as few strokes as possible. The format at the Olympic Games is stroke play, which consists of counting the number of strokes a golfer takes to complete an 18-hole course – played four times over four days. The player with the lowest cumulative stroke count at the end of the four rounds, emerges as the tournament winner.

In contrast to most ball games, golf does not use a standardized playing area, and adapting to the varied terrain encountered on different courses is a fundamental aspect of the game. Courses consist of 18 holes, each having a region of terrain containing a cup, which serves as the target for the ball. Every hole features a teeing ground to start from, and a putting green housing the cup. Along the route from the tee to the green, players encounter various standard forms of terrain, including the fairway, rough (tall grass), and hazards like water bodies, rocks, or sand-filled bunkers. The layout of each hole on a course is distinct and unique.

A total of 120 players (60 per gender) will compete at the 2024 Summer Olympics across **two medal events**:
- men's finals on Sunday, August 4 at 09:00
- women's finals on Saturday, August 10 at 09:00

The origins of golf are unclear and much debated. Traces of a similar sport played in the Netherlands can be found dating back to the 13th century. This version of the game involved using a club to strike a ball towards a target located several hundred yards away, with the winner determined by the fewest strokes taken. The term golf, or in Scots language *gowf*, is usually thought to be a Scots alteration of Dutch language *colf/kolf* or *colve/kolven* meaning stick, club, bat. This linguistic connection might suggest a link between early Dutch stick-and-ball games and the development of golf in Scotland.

Although stick-and-ball games have existed for centuries, it is generally accepted that modern golf developed in 15th century Scotland. Moreover, golf as we know it today, played over 18 holes, originated in Scotland, with the first codified rules written in 1754, in the town of St Andrews. The 18-hole round was created at the Old Course, also at St Andrews, in 1764. The world oldest golf tournament is The Open Championship, also known as the British Open, which was first played in 1860 at the Prestwick Golf Club in Ayrshire, Scotland.

Golf was featured in the Summer Olympic Games official program in 1900 and 1904. After an absence of 112 years, the sport made its Olympic comeback at the 2016 Rio de Janeiro Games in Brazil and was contested again at the Tokyo 2020 Olympic Games, held in 2021.

The inaugural Olympic champions in 1900 were from the USA, with Margaret Abbott clinching the women's title and Charles Sands securing the men's. Similarly, in the most recent Olympics in Tokyo, Nelly Korda and Xander Schauffele, both representing the USA, emerged victorious in the women's and men's tournaments, respectively.

HANDBALL

The handball tournaments at the 2024 Olympics will be held from July 25 to August 11. Preliminary pool matches will take place at South Paris Arena 6, with the final phase staged at Pierre Mauroy Stadium in Lille.

Handball involves two teams, each comprising seven players, including a goalkeeper, who use their hands to pass a ball with the aim of scoring by throwing it into the opposing goal. Players can take up to three steps without dribbling and are allowed to hold the ball for a maximum of three seconds. The modern version of the game is played on an indoor court measuring 40 by 20 meters (131 by 66 feet), featuring a goal positioned in the middle of each end. Surrounding the goals is a 6-meter (20 feet) zone exclusive to the defending goalkeeper; goals must be scored from outside this zone or while "diving" into it. A match consists of two periods of 30 minutes each, with victory going to the team that scores more goals. In the knockout phase, matches that end in a draw go into extra time (two halves of 5 minutes each) and potentially to a penalty shoot-out.

Handball is a contact sport where attackers and defenders are permitted to make body contact with an opponent, making it a very physical and demanding sport for the players involved. While protective equipment isn't mandatory, players may wear soft protective bands, pads, and mouth guards. Offensive strategies are strongly encouraged, as passive play is sanctioned. Endurance and strength are therefore essential attributes for players, alongside tactics, teamwork, and flexibility, as all players shift between offensive and defensive roles.

The sport is most popular in Europe, but it is also practiced in East Asia, North Africa, and parts of South America.

A total of 24 teams (12 women's and 12 men's) will compete for **two medal events**:
- women's finals on Saturday, August 10 at 15:00
- men's finals on Sunday, August 11 at 13:30

Games similar to handball were played in ancient Greece and are depicted on amphorae and stone carvings. While textual documentation is scarce, various accounts describe ball games involving players throwing the ball to one another, often to avoid interception by opposing team members. These games were played widely serving as both physical exercise and a social event.

Handball was first played towards the end of the 19th century in northern Europe: primarily in Denmark, Germany, Norway, and Sweden. The modern set of rules was published in 1917 in Berlin, which is seen as the official birth of the sport. The inaugural match took place in Germany that same year. Both versions of the sport were played until 1966, when indoor handball began to replace field handball.

Men's field handball, played outdoors, made its Olympic debut at the 1936 Berlin Games. It was also played as a demonstration sport during the Helsinki 1952 Olympics. Over the next several decades, indoor handball flourished and evolved in Scandinavian nations. The sport re-emerged onto the world stage, played indoor, at the 1972 Olympics in Munich. Subsequently, women's handball was introduced at the 1976 Games in Montreal. European nations have dominated this sport at the Olympics, with South Korea standing out as the only exception.

JUDO

Judo competitions consist of fourteen weight categories, evenly split with seven for women and seven for men. In each category, athletes are seeded in a single-elimination bracket, following a traditional knockout format until the final, with a slight twist. Those eliminated in the quarterfinals have the chance to compete through a repechage draw, contesting for a second bronze medal, thus resulting in double bronze medals awarded to the judokas. The mixed-team tournament, an event introduced in the previous edition, features a squad of six individual athletes, with three weight categories per gender, competing against another team. To secure victory in each match, the team must achieve four wins out of six rounds.

In judo, the objective is to throw your opponent to the ground, immobilize them with a pinning hold, or force them into submission with a joint lock or choke. There are two types of scores in judo.

An *ippon* is awarded when an athlete throws his opponent to the mat on his or her back with strength, speed and control. Ippon can also be awarded through submission, or by pinning an opponent to the ground for 20 seconds. If a judoka achieves ippon, they instantly win the match.

A *waza-ari* is awarded for a throw that isn't clear enough to be an ippon, either because is lacking speed or force, or if the opponent does not land primarily on their back. Waza-ari is also achieved when an opponent is pinned down for less than 20 seconds, but longer than 10 seconds. Two waza-ari in a match is the equivalent of an ippon and immediately ends the match.

A judo match lasts for four minutes, and if the score is tied at the end of this period, it enters overtime. Penalties are given for passiveness during matches or behavior that goes against the principles of judo.

A total of 372 judokas, with an equal distribution between men and women, will compete at the Games in Paris at Grand Palais Éphémère in *Champ de Mars* across **fifteen medal events**:
- women's 48 kg finals on Saturday, July 27 at 17:38
- men's 60 kg finals on Saturday, July 27 at 18:09
- men's 66 kg finals on Sunday, July 28 at 17:38
- women's 52 kg finals on Sunday, July 28 at 18:09
- women's 57 kg finals on Monday, July 29 at 17:38
- men's 73 kg finals on Monday, July 29 at 18:09
- men's 81 kg finals on Tuesday, July 30 at 17:38
- women's 63 kg finals on Tuesday, July 30 at 18:09
- women's 70 kg finals on Wednesday, July 31 at 17:38
- men's 90 kg finals on Wednesday, July 31 at 18:09
- men's 100 kg finals on Thursday, August 1 at 17:38
- women's 78 kg finals on Thursday, August 1 at 18:09
- women's +78 kg finals on Friday, August 2 at 17:38
- men's +100 kg finals on Friday, August 2 at 18:09
- mixed team finals on Saturday, August 3 at 17:20

Judo is a traditional Japanese martial art derived from jiu-jitsu, the hand-to-hand combat technique of ancient samurai warriors. Dr Kanō Jigorō, a Japanese educator, is the founder of the discipline in Tokyo, after opening his first *dojo* (school), the *kōdōkan*, in 1882.

Kanō began studying traditional Japanese jiu-jitsu in his youth, but found that many of its techniques were outdated and impractical for modern self-defense needs. He believed that martial arts training should be more than just combat techniques; it should also cultivate character, discipline, and mutual respect.

In Japanese, the word judo means "the gentle way", reflecting Kanō's emphasis on using an opponent's strength and momentum against them rather than relying solely on brute force. It's important to note that despite its gentle philosophy, judo requires considerable physical effort, highlighting the rigorous nature of the practice.

Dr. Kanō combined the philosophical principles of judo with physical, intellectual, and moral education methods while simultaneously eliminating many of the more dangerous aspects of jiu-jitsu. He structured judo training to include both *randori* (free practice) and *kata* (prearranged forms), providing students with a well-rounded understanding of the art.

Judo became popular in Europe and particularly France in the late 20th century, becoming the first martial art widely practiced outside of Japan.

There were no weight categories in Judo until the 1930s. In fact, the introduction of weight divisions faced significant opposition due to concerns that it might compromise the skillful essence of Judo. Before that, everyone fought everyone and weight differences were not considered important.

The first time judo was seen in the Olympic Games was in an informal demonstration hosted by Dr. Kanō himself, at the 1932 Los Angeles Games.

Judo made its Olympic debut at Tokyo 1964. It was a men-only discipline and there were just four weight classes: lightweight up to 63 kg, middleweight up to 80 kg, heavyweight up to 93 kg, and openweight. Judo was dropped for the 1968 Olympics, but became a permanent fixture of the program since the 1972 Games in Munich.

The women's competition was introduced at the Olympics in 1988 as a demonstration sport, though it became an official medal event just four years later at the Barcelona 1992 Games.

Since its inclusion in the Olympics, judo has experienced a surge in global popularity, evidenced by the participation of 128 nations in the judo competition at the 2020 Tokyo Games. Japan has been a formidable force in this sport at the Olympics, with Japanese judokas securing an impressive total of 96 medals (48 gold, 21 silver, and 27 bronze). They are followed by the French athletes, who have earned 57 medals (16 gold, 13 silver, and 28 bronze) and judokas from South Korea with 46 medals (11 gold, 17 silver, and 18 bronze) to their credit.

MARATHON SWIMMING

Marathon swimming races take place in open water environments such as the sea, rivers, and lakes. Athletes are required to complete a 10-kilometer course, which takes nearly two hours to swim. Their endurance, physical strength, and mental power are all put to the test during this challenging event. Adaptability is also crucial in marathon swimming. Tides and currents in open water can change quickly, requiring athletes to adjust their strategies accordingly. Using the right tactics for the course and conditions is therefore essential. During the final 3 kilometers of the race, swimmers begin to position themselves for the finish line. How they manage their efforts during this final phase vastly impacts the end result.

While marathon foot-races have a precisely defined distance, marathon swims vary in length. A commonly accepted minimum distance is 10 kilometers (6.21 miles), which is the range of the marathon swimming event at the Olympic Games.

The triple crown of open water swimming includes three renowned marathon swims: 21 miles (34 kilometers) across the English Channel, 20.1 miles (32.3 kilometers) between Catalina Island and the mainland in Southern California, USA, and 28.5 miles (45.9 kilometers) around Manhattan Island in New York City, USA.

In total, 44 swimmers (22 of each gender) will compete at Pont Alexandre III through the Seine River in Paris across **two medal events**:
- women's finals on Thursday, August 8 at 07:30
- men's finals on Friday, August 9 at 07:30

One of the earliest marathon swims dates back to 1875 when Matthew Webb achieved the remarkable feat of becoming the first person to swim across the English Channel. Similarly, a pivotal moment in marathon swimming history occurred in 1926 when Gertrude Ederle, at the age of 19, made waves by becoming the first woman to conquer the English Channel. She shattered the existing world record for the crossing by employing the crawl stroke technique.

During the initial three editions of the modern Olympic Games, all swimming events took place in natural bodies of water, as pools were not available until 1908. Open water competitions resurfaced in 1991 with the introduction of marathon swimming at the world championships. Initially, these events were held over 25 kilometers and often took more than five hours to complete. The first 10-kilometer race was held at the world swimming championships in Fukuoka, Japan, in 2001.

Marathon swimming is the most recent swimming discipline to be added to the Olympic program, with the 10-kilometer (6.21 miles) race debuting at the Beijing Games in 2008. The Netherlands is the only country to have won three gold medals in this discipline, with Germany, Hungary, Brazil, Russia, and Tunisia claiming the other gold medals awarded thus far.

MODERN PENTATHLON

The modern pentathlon events in 2024 Games are scheduled between August 8 and 11. Fencing will take place at North Paris Arena, while the other events are staged at Château de Versailles.

Modern pentathlon consists of four events combining five sports: épée fencing, 200 meters (656.2 feet) freestyle swimming, riding, pistol shooting, and a 3.2 kilometers (1.988 miles) cross-country run.

The competition is divided into two sections: the initial three events (fencing, swimming, and riding) are evaluated using a points system. The laser-run is the final combined event (pistol shooting and cross-country running), based on the points won in the first three events.

Fencing comprises two rounds: a ranking round where each athlete engages in bouts against one another, lasting a minute or until the first hit. This is followed by a second round based on the results of the initial one, with a single-elimination format, where each bout lasts 45 seconds. Points are granted for every bout won.

In the 200-meter freestyle race in swimming, points are awarded based on the achieved time.

The riding event features a show jumping course with twelve obstacles, on an unfamiliar horse that the athlete is allocated in a draw just 20 minutes before competing. Scores are based on penalties for fallen bars, refusals, falls, and exceeding the time limit.

Points accumulated from the first three disciplines are converted into a time handicap for the final combined event, comprising pistol shooting and cross-country running. The competitor in the lead starts first, while the other participants begin with a delayed start based on their points deficit.

The running and pistol shooting events are combined in the laser-run: athletes will face four rounds of shooting, each followed by an 800-meter (874.9 yards) run. In every round, they fire laser pistols at targets situated 10 meters away. Competitors must hit five targets, or allow 50 seconds to elapse before they can move to the next leg of the run; there is no additional penalty for missed shots. Because the contestants have staggered starts based on the initial three events, the first athlete to cross the finish line in the laser-run wins the gold medal. This sport is exceptionally demanding, challenging athletes both mentally and physically, requiring a wide range of skills due to the diverse nature of its events.

A total of 72 athletes (36 women and 36 men) will compete for **two medal events**:
- men's finals on Saturday, August 10 at 19:10
- women's finals on Sunday, August 11 at 12:40

The modern pentathlon is the successor to the ancient pentathlon, which comprised running, jumping, javelin, discus, and wrestling. Baron Pierre de Coubertin, founder of the modern Olympics, highly appreciated the pentathlon of the ancient Games. He proposed a similar competition that would test the strengths of a "complete" athlete, but involve more modern disciplines.

Modern pentathlon was introduced to the Olympic program in 1912. Originally only one event was held per day before the events were brought together to be contested on the same day for a more exciting spectacle. The women's event was introduced at the 2000 Games in Sydney. Throughout its Olympic history, European athletes have consistently excelled in the modern pentathlon, with Hungary and Sweden notably dominating the discipline.

RHYTHMIC GYMNASTICS

The rhythmic gymnastics events in Paris are scheduled between August 8 and 10 at *La Chapelle* Arena.

Rhythmic gymnastics is expression through movement, blending elements of traditional dance with the grace and athleticism of artistic gymnastics. Central for the routine are the four apparatus utilized: ribbon, hoop, ball, and clubs. The accompanying music, with vocals allowed, serves as a significant role, enhancing the gymnasts' performances.

At the international level, rhythmic gymnastics is a women-only discipline.

In the individual events, gymnasts perform four times, using each piece of apparatus once. Every routine must be 75 to 90 seconds long.

In group events, teams of five gymnasts perform twice: the first routine involves one set of apparatus, while the second exercise includes two different apparatus.

The performance is evaluated using a combination of the D-score (difficulty / content of the exercise), the A score (artistry), and the E score (execution).

This sport incorporates elements of gymnastics, dance, and calisthenics, necessitating athletes to embody strength, flexibility, agility, dexterity, and coordination. Throughout routines, gymnasts execute leaps, balances, rotations, and elaborate maneuvers of their chosen apparatus, captivating audiences with their skill and grace.

In total, 94 gymnasts (24 individual athletes and 14 groups of five athletes) will compete in Paris across **two medal events**:
- women's individual finals on Friday, August 9 at 14:30
- women's group finals on Saturday, August 10 at 14:00

Gymnastics is one of the oldest sports that is still practiced today with origins that date back to ancient civilization. Remarkably, the International Gymnastics Federation, founded in 1881, holds the distinction of being the oldest international sports federation in the world.

Rhythmic gymnastics, on the other hand, is a far newer discipline of the sport, as it evolved from the mass gymnastics popular in Europe in the late 19th and early 20th centuries. Competitive rhythmic gymnastics began in the 1940s primarily within the Soviet Union. It was officially recognized as a discipline in 1961, first as modern gymnastics, then as rhythmic sportive gymnastics and finally as rhythmic gymnastics. The inaugural world championships took place in Budapest in 1963.

Rhythmic gymnastics became an Olympic sport in 1984 Games in Los Angeles, with the individual all-around event. The group event was introduced 12 years later at the Atlanta Olympics.

Eastern European countries, particularly Russia, have significantly dominated the sport. In fact, Russia has taken home 10 out of 17 gold medals on offer since rhythmic gymnastics joined the Olympic program. Outside of the Eastern European sphere, only a select few nations – Spain, Canada, and Israel, have managed to challenge their supremacy and take home gold medals at the Olympics.

ROWING

The rowing competitions at the 2024 Olympics will take place from July 27 to August 3 at the National Olympic Nautical Stadium of Île-de-France in *Vaires-sur-Marne*.

Rowing, sometimes called crew in the United States, is the sport of racing boats propelled by oars. Unlike paddling sports, where paddles are not attached to the boat, rowing utilizes oars secured by oarlocks. Additionally, rowers sit with their backs to the direction of movement, allowing them to use their powerful leg muscles more effectively and synchronize their strokes with greater precision.

Rowing is divided into two disciplines: double scull and sweep rowing. In sweep events, rowers hold a single oar with both hands, while in sculling they hold two oars, one in each hand.

The rowing program for the Olympics features a total of fourteen events, seven each for both women and men in identical boat classes. Sculling events include singles, doubles, lightweight doubles (weight restricted), and quads. Sweep events include coxless pairs, coxless fours, and eights. The eight-person crews have a coxswain, who steers the boat and directs the crew. The boat is steered using a small rudder that is attached to the foot of one of the rowers by a cable. Rowers compete on calm water course across a distance of 2,000 meters (1.2 miles) with several lanes marked using buoys.

As mentioned before, there is weight restricted category, known as lightweight rowing. In this event, there are limits placed on the maximum body weight of competitors, to encourage more universality in this sport. These limits are: crew average 70 kg (154.3 lb) – no rower over 72.5 kg (159.8 lb) for men and crew average 57 kg (125.7 lb) – no rower over 59 kg (130.1 lb) for women.

Olympic rowers must possess outstanding physical fitness and technical expertise, including proper stroke mechanics, blade work, body positioning, and boat handling. Furthermore, in crew competitions, they must demonstrate exceptional teamwork, synchronization, and coordination skills.

A total of 502 rowers, with an equal distribution between men and women, will compete at the Games in Paris across **fourteen medal events**:
- men's quad. sculls finals on Wednesday, July 31 at 12:26
- women's quad. sculls finals on Wednesday, July 31 at 12:38
- women's double sculls finals on Thursday, August 1 at 11:18
- men's double sculls finals on Thursday, August 1 at 11:30
- women's four finals on Thursday, August 1 at 11:50
- men's four finals on Thursday, August 1 at 12:10
- men's pair finals on Friday, August 2 at 11:30
- women's pair finals on Friday, August 2 at 11:42
- lightweight men's double sculls finals on Friday, August 2 at 12:02
- lightweight women's double sculls finals on Friday, August 2 at 12:22
- women's single sculls finals on Saturday, August 3 at 10:18
- men's single sculls finals on Saturday, August 3 at 10:30
- women's eight finals on Saturday, August 3 at 10:50
- men's eight finals on Saturday, August 3 at 11:10

Rowing originally served as a means of transport in ancient Egypt, Greece and Rome. In the 13th century, Venetian festivals called *regata* included boat races. The origins of modern competitive rowing can be traced back to the early 17th century, when professional watermen organized races, known as regattas, on the River Thames in London, England. Amateur rowing competitions began to emerge towards the end of the 18th century with the establishment of "boat clubs" at British schools. The first major rowing competition was the now-annual Oxford and Cambridge Boat Race which began in 1829. The Harvard–Yale Regatta is the oldest intercollegiate sporting event in the United States, having been contested since 1852.

Rowing has been part of the Summer Olympics since its debut in 1900. It was also on the program at the 1896 Games, but was canceled due to bad weather. Women's events were introduced at the 1976 Games in Montreal, marking the end of exclusive male participation. This addition increased the growth of women's rowing, encouraging national federations to support women's events. In 1996, lightweight rowing events, featuring weight-limited crews, were added to the Olympic program.

The current standard course of 2,000 meters was not always used. The distance was different in Paris in 1900 (1,750 meters), in St. Louis in 1904 (3218 meters), in London in 1908 (2,412 meters), and also in London 1948 (1,850 meters). Initially, women's races covered a distance of 1,000 meters until it was extended to 2,000 meters in 1988.

Early Olympic rowing events featured match races involving two or three boats, until the modern six-boat side-by-side format first adopted in the 1936 Games. The only exception was the 1952 Olympics, which featured races with four or five boats, but since then, the six-boat format has been standard.

Several other boat classes have appeared in multiple Olympic Games, but were subsequently removed, particularly those with coxswains. Examples include the men's coxed pair and coxed four (1900–1992), women's coxed four (1976–1988) and women's coxed quad. sculls (1976–1984). The eights remain the only class that has consistently featured coxswains.

The United States leads the Olympic rowing medal table with a total of 89 medals, comprising 33 gold, 32 silver, and 24 bronze medals. The best all-time performing rower at the Olympic Games is Romanian Elisabeta Lipă who won eight medals (five golds, two silvers, one bronze) between 1984–2000. The highest ranked male is British rower Steve Redgrave with six medals (five golds – won at five consecutive Olympics and one bronze).

Henry 'Bobby' Pearce's place in sporting history is largely attributed to his achievement of becoming the first singles sculler to win consecutive Olympic gold medals. Still, he was also celebrated thanks to a memorable incident during the Amsterdam Olympics of 1928.

In his quarter-final race, Pearce found himself in the lead when he encountered an unexpected obstacle: a family of ducks crossing the Stoten Canal directly in his path. Rather than plow through and risk harming them, Pearce leaned on his oars and waited until the ducks had safely cleared the way. This allowed his French opponent to catch up and even pull ahead to a five-length lead. In spite of that, Pearce managed to regain his momentum, winning the race and ultimately the Olympic final. His gesture towards the ducks made him an instant favorite with the schoolchildren of Netherlands.

RUGBY SEVENS

The rugby sevens tournaments at the 2024 Olympics are scheduled to run from July 24 to 30 at Stade de France in Paris.

Although plenty of rugby variants have emerged over the years—including league, beach, and flag—the two main forms of the game remain 15-player union and sevens. Rugby is played with an oval-shaped ball, primarily using hands.

Teams aim to score points by carrying, passing, kicking, or grounding the ball in the opponent's end zone, called the try zone. Points can also be scored through penalty kicks and conversions. Both variants share the same basic rules for tackling, backward passes, and scrums, but differ based on the number of players on the pitch, 7 instead of 15.

Rugby sevens is fast-paced and intense, on a field of the same dimensions as the 15 player game, played in matches lasting 14 minutes (seven-minute halves). It is an exceptionally testing version of the sport, in which players make more sprints and score more tries than in rugby union. Sevens scores are generally comparable to regular 15-player, but scoring occurs much more frequently in sevens, since the defenders are more spaced out. Points are earned in the same way as in rugby union: 5 for a try, 2 for a conversion, and 3 for a drop goal or penalty.

The game is popular at all levels, with amateur and club tournaments typically held in the summer months. It is one of the most widely played forms of rugby globally, enjoying popularity in various regions including Africa, Asia, Europe, the Americas, and especially in the South Pacific.

A total of 24 teams (12 women's and 12 men's) will compete for **two medal events**:
- men's finals on Saturday, July 27 at 19:45
- women's finals on Tuesday, July 30 at 19:45

The sport of rugby traces its roots back to medieval times across various European countries, but it was between 1845 and 1848 that the foundations of modern rugby codes were laid by students from a school in the English town of Rugby and the University of Cambridge.

Rugby sevens was initially conceived in 1883 by Ned Haig and David Sanderson, both butchers from Melrose, Scotland, as a fundraising initiative for their local club, Melrose RFC. The inaugural rugby sevens match took place at The Greenyards, the Melrose ground, and received a positive response. The tradition continues with the annual Melrose Sevens tournament still being played today.

Rugby's presence at the Olympic Games spans several eras. A men's rugby union competition was first included at the 1900 Paris Games, and was contested again at the 1908, 1920, and 1924 Olympics. The sport was dropped from the Olympic program following the 1924 Games in Paris.

In 2016, rugby sevens was contested in the Rio de Janeiro Olympics for the first time and it has been part of the men's and women's program since. While Fiji has secured both men's titles so far, the women's competition was initially won by Australia in 2016, followed by New Zealand in 2020.

SAILING

Sailing competitions at the 2024 Games are scheduled to be held from July 28 to August 8 at Marseille Marina, since Paris is not a seaport.

Sailing involves moving a boat solely by harnessing the power of the wind. Mastery over ever-changing conditions requires both great skill and experience on the part of the athletes. At the Olympics, competitions are made up of fleet racing, where only boats of the exact same model will compete against each other around the same varied course. The various sailing disciplines are constantly changing and boats are designed to be increasingly small and lightweight, placing ever greater demands on both the athletic and technical capacities of the sailors. Competition is divided into men's, women's, and mixed categories.

The Olympic sailing events feature these boat types: dinghies, skiffs, and multihulls.

"Dinghy" is a broad term historically used to refer to any type of sailboat or rowboat. Today, there are several categories of dinghies sailed at the Olympics with different sizes, speeds, and number of sailors to man them. The dinghies currently used in Olympic competitions are: the ILCA 7, ILCA 6, and 470.

➢ The ILCA 7 is the Standard Laser rig and has been used as the Olympic men's one person dinghy since 1996. A small single handed dinghy, the Laser is one of the most popular boats in the world, due to its broad accessibility and simplicity to set up and sail. It has a single mainsail, meaning it is lightweight and fast to sail.

➢ The ILCA is the Laser Radial rig, used as the Olympic women's one person dinghy since 2008. The ILCA 6 features the same fiberglass hull as the ILCA 7, but with a slightly shorter and more flexible mast and 18% less sail area.

➢ The 470, named after the overall length of the boat at 4.70 meters (470 centimeters), is a double-handed monohull planing dinghy. These boats are rigged with a mainsail, jib, and spinnaker. Unlike the ILCA 6 and 7, the 470 is sailed with trapeze at the Olympic level. Teamwork is key to success in this boat as the optimum weight for the crew is between 120-135 kilograms. The 470 has been an Olympic class since Montreal 1976, when it was an open class. The first ever women's - only sailing event at the Olympics took place in 1988, when it was divided into men's and women's classes. At Paris 2024, it will become a mixed dinghy event.

Sailors distinguish between "skiffs" and "high-performance dinghies". Skiffs are the quickest kind of dinghy, characterized by flat and narrow hulls (the part of the boat that sits on the water) and large, asymmetrical foresails (called spinnakers). While high-performance dinghies are also built for speed and racing, they tend to have more rounded hulls and symmetrical foresails. The skiffs featured in current Olympic competitions are the 49er and 49erFX.

➢ The 49er, named after its hull length of 4.99 meters, is a two-handed high-performance skiff. It is rigged with three sails: a main sail, a jib, and an asymmetrical spinnaker. The 49er men's double-handed skiff has been an Olympic class boat since 2000. The two sailors onboard take different roles; the helm generally makes the tactical decisions and steers the boat, while the crew undertakes more of the physical work and controls the sails. Both of the crew are equipped with their own trapeze, and sail while cantilevered over the water to the fullest extent, to balance against the sails. The mast can support a combined crew weight of up to 165 kilograms from its dual trapeze.

➢ The 49erFX is a redesigned version of the 49er, made to better suit the weight of all-female crews. The hull is the same as the 49er, but the mast and sail plan were designed with the aim of developing a skiff to provide the correct amount of power for the lighter crew target weight. This was achieved with a scaled-down rig, which can be adjusted for optimum performance in a variety of conditions. It was first selected as the women's double-handed skiff for Rio de Janeiro 2016.

A multihull, as the name indicates, is a boat with more than one hull, for example, a catamaran which has two hulls. At the Olympics the Nacra 17 is the multihull currently used.
➢ The Nacra 17 is a high-performance catamaran and gets its name from being 17 feet long. It features hydrofoil daggerboards and winglets on the bottom of the rudders. Light in weight, it has been designed to cut through the water with minimum drag and maximum stability, it is an agile but challenging boat to sail. When fully foiling, a fleet of Nacra 17s soaring above the water as they race around the course is a sight to behold. The mixed multihull event was actually the first mixed discipline on the Olympic sailing program and made its debut at the Rio de Janeiro Games in 2016.

Besides boat races, there are also board-based sailing events at the Olympics.
➢ Windsurfing, a combination of surfing and sailing, became an Olympic event in 1984. The current windsurfing equipment utilized in the Olympics is the iQFoil. In Paris 2024, the iQFoil will replace the RS:X in both the women's and men's windsurfing class. The sail size is nine square meters for men and eight square meters for women.
➢ Kiteboarding is a new addition to the Olympic sailing program for 2024. This discipline requires athletes to navigate across the water on a board similar to a wakeboard, using a hand-controlled kite for propulsion. In Paris 2024, both women and men kiteboarding will compete using the Formula Kite equipment, which features a hydrofoil board and foil kite.

Each event is divided into opening heats and medal races. Depending on the event, the number of races in the opening heats varies. In dinghy racing there are 10, in skiff and multihull 12 races. Windsurfers need 20 and kitesurfers 16 before they can compete for a medal. After the opening heats, only the top 10 finishers are allowed to take part in the medal race. In windsurfing and kitesurfing the rules are different, with more direct eliminations.

A number of 330 sailors, with an equal distribution between men and women, will compete across **ten** different **medal events**:
- men's skiff 49er finals on Thursday, August 1
- women's skiff 49er FX finals on Thursday, August 1
- women's windsurfing IQFoil finals on Friday, August 2
- men's windsurfing IQFoil finals on Friday, August 2
- women's dinghy ILCA 6 finals on Tuesday, August 6
- men's dinghy ILCA 7 finals on Tuesday, August 6
- mixed multihull Nacra 17 finals on Wednesday, August 7
- mixed dinghy 470 finals on Wednesday, August 7
- men's kite Formula Kite finals on Thursday, August 8
- women's kite Formula Kite finals on Thursday, August 8

In ancient times, sailing was associated with the privileged classes across Egypt, Rome, Greece, and Asia. Although these civilizations sailed the seas and oceans with large vessels, it wasn't until the 17th century that it was practiced as a sport in the Netherlands. Using boats that measured up to 65 feet, the Dutch would compete with these vessels before races arrived in England and eventually expanded to the American colonies. That was when sailing became an actual sport.

International races began in 1851 when members of the New York Yacht Club decided to take part in a competition in England. To compete, they built a 101-foot schooner named America, sailed to England and won a trophy called the Hundred Guineas Cup. The trophy was then renamed The America's Cup in memory of this first international sailing competition. Today, this race remains the oldest competition in the world and arguably one of the most prestigious international events in the world of sport sailing.

Sailing was first contested at the 1900 Olympic Games, after bad weather canceled the races for what would have been its Olympic debut in 1896. The sport has appeared in every Olympics since, with the exception of 1904.

Interestingly, the sport was not known as Sailing at the Games until Sydney 2000 – it was called Yachting up until then, and became the first Olympic sport to make a name change.

In the early Olympic Games, sailing was dominated by bigger boats, sometimes with as many as 10-12 sailors, and time handicaps were used to adjudicate the races. Initially, the boat classes were specified in tons, then later in meters, feet or generic names. Starting from 1924, and increasingly from the 1950s onward, the trend has been towards smaller one-design boats with fewer crew members. In the last 20 years, equipment trials have resulted in several new boats reflecting the latest developments in the sport.

During the 2008 Beijing Games, only one event had a three-person crew, with five events contested by lone sailors. The line-up of classes at Tokyo 2020 was a suitable mixture of older boats with rich history, such as the Finn and the 470, those reflecting the design and technology advances in the sport, like the 49er/49erFX and the Nacra 17, and modern disciplines like windsurfing. Paris 2024 will build on this legacy and introduces new equipment with kiteboarding represented for the first time and foiling in half of the events.

Women have always been allowed to compete in Olympic sailing alongside men, with the exception of the post-World War II 1948 Olympics where it was decided the events should only be open to male sailors. Remarkably, the first ever woman to win an Olympic gold medal was a sailor. At Paris 1900, Hélène de Pourtalès, representing Switzerland, was a crew member on board Lérina, which won gold in the first race and silver in the second race in the 1-to-2-ton class. In 1988, separate sailing events were introduced exclusively for women.

At the top of the Olympic sailing medal table is Great Britain, conquering a total of 64 medals, including 31 gold, 21 silver, and 12 bronze. It is followed by the United States, with a total of 61 medals, comprised of 19 gold, 23 silver, and 19 bronze.

SHOOTING

Shooting events at the 2024 Games will take place at the National Shooting Center in Châteauroux.

At the Summer Olympics it comprises fifteen medal events, covering seven disciplines. These are evenly distributed between rifle, pistol, and shotgun with five events each.

The rifle used is single-loaded with a 5.6-millimeter caliber, consistent across all rifle events. For the 10 meters air pistol event, a 4.5-millimeter caliber single-loaded pistol is utilized. The 25 meters men's event involves a rapid fire pistol with a five-shot magazine, also in a 5.6 caliber.

Shotguns used in the Olympics are 12-gauge with an 18.5-millimeter caliber. In firearms, the gauge serves as a unit of measurement. In shotguns, the gauge is determined by the number of equally weighing spherical balls made from a pound of lead that can be fit inside the gun barrel.

Rifle and pistol competitions take place on shooting ranges, with targets placed at distances of 10, 25, and 50 meters. Athletes adopt three positions: kneeling (where the athlete goes down on one knee and rests the elbow on the other knee), prone, and standing, with some events incorporating all positions. Marksmen use relaxation techniques to lower their heartbeat, aiming to hit the targets as accurately and as close to the center (the bullseye) as possible.

Contrarily, shotgun events unfold outdoors, involving shooting at flying targets measuring just 10 centimeters in diameter, fired at speeds exceeding 100 kilometers per hour from diverse angles and trajectories. Mastery in this discipline demands a great deal of concentration, quick decision-making, and sharp reflexes.

In the Olympic Games, the shooting sport has always enjoyed the distinction of awarding the first medals of the Games.

A total of 340 athletes, with an equal distribution between men and women, will compete across **fifteen medal events**:
- mixed team 10 m air rifle finals on Saturday, July 27 at 11:00
- men's 10 m air pistol finals on Sunday, July 28 at 09:30
- women's 10 m air pistol finals on Sunday, July 28 at 12:00
- women's 10 m air rifle finals on Monday, July 29 at 09:30
- men's 10 m air rifle finals on Monday, July 29 at 12:00
- mixed team 10 m air pistol finals on Tuesday, July 30 at 10:00
- men's trap finals on Tuesday, July 30 at 15:30
- women's trap finals on Wednesday, July 31 at 15:30
- men's 50 m rifle 3 positions finals on Thursday, August 1 at 09:30
- women's 50 m rifle 3 positions finals on Friday, August 2 at 09:30
- women's 25 m pistol finals on Saturday, August 3 at 09:30
- men's skeet finals on Saturday, August 3 at 15:30
- women's skeet finals on Sunday, August 4 at 15:30
- men's 25 m rapid fire pistol finals on Monday, August 5 at 09:30
- mixed team skeet finals on Monday, August 5 at 15:00

Shooting sports have a long history, evolving from their origins in military training to become popular recreational and competitive activities. Shooting has been an Olympic sport since the first modern Games and has been practiced in Europe for centuries, with some German clubs dating back more than five hundred years. These activities grew in popularity in English-speaking countries, particularly with the formation of the National Rifle Association in the United States in 1871. Today, shooting is a popular sport worldwide, with athletes from over 100 countries participating in shooting events at each Olympic Games.

French pistol champion and pioneer of the modern Olympics, Pierre de Coubertin, actively participated in many of these early competitions. His involvement significantly contributed to the inclusion of five shooting events in the 1896 Olympics. Except for the 1904 and 1928 Games, shooting sports have been a consistent feature at every Summer Olympics since Athens in 1896.

Over time, the events have undergone several changes to keep up with technology and social standards. Targets, once resembling humans or animals in appearance and size, have transitioned to a circular shape to avoid associating the sport with any form of violence. Additionally, some events have been dropped, while new ones have been introduced to the Olympic shooting program.

Events marked as 'men's' were technically open events from 1968 to 1980 (and in shotgun events until 1992), although very few women took part in them. Despite this, two women achieved notable success in these events: Margaret Murdock from the USA won silver in rifle 3 positions in 1976 and Zhang Shan, representing China, claimed gold in skeet in 1992. Margaret Murdock's silver at the 1976 Games made her the first markswoman in history to win an Olympic medal. Murdock's accomplishment preceded the introduction of three separate women's events at the 1984 Games in Los Angeles: air rifle, three-position rifle, and sport pistol. Thus, from only five women who competed at the 1980 Olympics, the subsequent Games in Los Angeles, which introduced these women-only events, featured 77 female participants. Since 1984, the number has seen an increase, resulting in gender parity between women and men.

The United States has won by far the most Olympic medals, 116 (57 gold, 31 silver, and 28 bronze), followed by China with a total of 67 medals (26 gold, 16 silver, and 25 bronze).

In the early days of competitions some events were featured, now considered at the very least unusual, such as live pigeon shooting in 1900. Participants in these events aimed to take down as many live pigeons as possible. Birds were released individually from 'traps' positioned in front of the shooters and winners were determined by the number of birds successfully shot down. A shooter was eliminated once they missed two birds. Nearly 300 pigeons were killed during this event, marking the first and only time in Olympic history where animals were killed on purpose. Subsequently, animal rights campaigns were mounted to stop this practice, leading to the prohibition of live shooting. In 1902, bans came into force in the United States leading to the introduction of 'clay pigeons' as substitutes. Notably, the results of this event are not included in the official Olympic records.

SKATEBOARDING

Skateboarding competitions at the 2024 Summer Olympics are scheduled to run from July 27 to August 7 at the famous *Place de La Concorde* in the heart of the French capital.

Skateboarding is a dynamic sport that involves riding and performing tricks on a skateboard. Athletes use their boards to navigate various terrain, including streets, skate parks, ramps, and other urban environments. Skateboarders perform tricks such as ollies, kickflips, grinds, and aerial maneuvers, showcasing their skill, creativity, and style. This sport is characterized by its individualistic nature, with participants often developing their unique tricks and personal flair.

The world's greatest skateboarders will face each other at the Olympic Games, competing in the two most popular and spectacular disciplines: park and street. Athletes will showcase their most impressive tricks, meeting criteria for the degree of difficulty, speed, and range of moves. The events consist of two rounds: prelims and finals.

In the park competition, athletes navigate a diverse course featuring bowls and numerous bends, utilizing them to gain speed and perform tricks mid-air. Judges evaluate skateboarders based on the height and speed of their aerial maneuvers, as well as their capacity to utilize the entire surface and all its obstacles. Competitors perform three 45-second runs, with their best run out of three counting towards their final score.

Street events take place on a straight 'street-like' course with stairs, handrails and short ramps set up to resemble the urban environments where skateboarding started out. Athletes perform a range of tricks and are also judged on how they control their board during the two 45-second runs and five tricks they carry out.

At the 2024 Games, 88 skateboarders will face each other in **four medal events**:
- men's street finals on Saturday, July 27 at 17:00
- women's street finals on Sunday, July 28 at 17:00
- women's park finals on Tuesday, August 6 at 17:30
- men's park finals on Wednesday, August 7 at 17:30

Skateboarding is a young and spectacular sport that developed in the United States in the 1950s, as surf culture was taking off. It was then part of the underground, alternative culture of the 1980s, going hand in hand with the values of freedom, rebellion, and thrill-seeking. The sport continued to develop and became more widely accessible at the start of the 21st century, proving a huge hit among younger audiences.

After its Olympic debut at the Tokyo 2020 Games, skateboarding will once again be on the program for Paris. Japanese athletes claimed victory in three out of the four medal events awarded in Tokyo. Sakura Yosozumi triumphed in the women's park competition. Momiji Nishiya, at the remarkable age of 13, secured gold in the women's street competition, while Yuto Horigome clinched the top spot in the men's street competition. The other gold medal was captured by Australia's Keegan Palmer in the men's park event.

SOCCER / FOOTBALL

The 2024 soccer or football tournaments are scheduled to take place between July 24 and August 10 in France. Alongside the Olympic host city of Paris, matches will be held in Bordeaux, Lyon, Marseille, Nantes, Nice, and Saint-Étienne. Both finals will be played at the Parc des Princes stadium.

Football, known as soccer in North America, is a team sport involving two lineups of 11 players each, aiming to score more goals than their opponents. The game is divided into two 45-minute halves, and matches can end in a draw. During the knockout phase, if a match ends in a draw, it goes into extra time consisting of two 15-minute halves. If the score remains tied after extra time, the match proceeds to a penalty shootout.

Players primarily use their feet to control, pass, and shoot the ball. They may also use their head, chest, and legs, but not their hands or arms, except for the goalkeeper within their penalty area. Each team consists of one goalkeeper and ten outfield players, who play as defenders (central defenders or full-backs/wing-backs), midfielders (defensive, offensive, or wide midfielders), and forwards (wingers or strikers).

For the Olympics, men's squads are restricted to under-23 players, (born on or after 1 January 2001), with a maximum of three overage players allowed. There are no age restrictions for women's squads.

A total of 28 teams (12 women's and 16 men's) will compete for **two medal events**:
- men's finals on Friday, August 9 at 18:00
- women's finals on Saturday, August 10 at 17:00

The history of soccer stretches back to eighth-century England, where some version of the game was played. Predecessors of soccer may trace back to ancient China, during the Han dynasty. The earliest form of the game appeared as an exercise in a military manual dating back to the 2nd and 3rd centuries BC. In this game, named *cuju* or *tsu' chu*, meaning "kick ball", players could use any part of the body apart from hands. The objective was to kick a ball filled with feathers and hair through an opening measuring only 30-40 centimeters in width, into a small net fixed onto long bamboo canes.

In medieval England, large crowds of people would gather to drag a pig's bladder to markers situated at opposing ends of a town, in order to score. Such events were well known for being as violent as they were popular. In the 16th century, English schools began establishing modern codes, transforming the game from chaotic mob events into a proper sport. The modern game of soccer originated in the mid-19th century in an effort to standardize the diverse variations played in English schools, ultimately leading to the formulation of the Laws of the Game in 1863.

Soccer was an early addition to the Olympic program, debuting at the Paris Games in 1900, and has been played at every edition, except for the 1932 Games, when it was omitted to promote the newly established soccer World Cup tournament. Historically, European teams dominated the sport until 1992, when Spain became the last nation to clinch the gold medal in men's soccer. Since the 1996 Games, African and Latin American teams have won every gold medal.

Women's soccer made its Olympic debut in Atlanta in 1996. Since then, the USA women's team has been highly successful, securing victory multiple times, in 1996, 2004, 2008, and 2012. Canada is the women's defending champions, while Brazil, the two-time defending Olympic champions failed to qualify.

SPORT CLIMBING

Competition climbing at the 2024 Games will be held from the August 5 to 10 at Le Bourget Climbing Venue in Saint-Denis.

The Olympic schedule comprises three formats: bouldering, speed, and lead. The total number of medal events in sport climbing will double from two in the previous edition, separating the boulder-and-lead tandem from the speed format.

In bouldering, athletes climb 4.5 meters high walls without ropes, within a limited time frame and with the fewest attempts possible.

In the lead event, athletes ascend as high as possible on a wall over 15 meters high within six minutes, without prior knowledge of the route. The routes for this event progressively become more complex and challenging, requiring all of the athletes' physical and mental ability.

Speed climbing is a thrilling race against the clock, with competitors facing off in one-on-one elimination rounds. The best athletes scale a 15-meter-high, five-degree inclined wall in under six seconds for men and under seven seconds for women, combining precision and explosiveness.

In Tokyo 2020, each athlete competed in all three disciplines and their final scores were based on the combined results of the three competitions. Paris 2024 will see some changes, with two competitions crowning their own Olympic champions. One will be a combined competition of bouldering and lead events, while the other will only feature the speed event.

A number of 68 climbers will compete across **four medal events**:
- women's speed finals on Wednesday, August 7 at 12:55
- men's speed finals on Thursday, August 8 at 12:55
- men's boulder & lead finals on Friday, August 9 at 10:15 & 12:28
- women's boulder & lead finals on Saturday, August 10 at 10:15 & 12:28

Sport climbing has emerged as a modern sport that has become immensely popular over the past two decades. It represents a youthful and inclusive activity, with 39 percent of climbers being under the age of 18. Practiced both in natural outdoor settings and within urban indoor facilities, sport climbing boasts a global following, with over 25 million enthusiasts in 150 countries worldwide.

In 1985, a group of climbers gathered in Bardonecchia, near Turin, Italy, for an event called "SportRoccia." This marked the inaugural organized lead competition, where participants ascended within a certain time limit. The following year saw the organization of the first competition on an artificial climbing wall, held in Vaulx-en-Velin near Lyon, France.

Sport climbing took its first steps on the Olympic stage at the Buenos Aires *Youth* Olympic Games, in 2018. While the event wasn't extensively promoted, the public was captivated by the spectacle and suspense of this thrilling sport. A hit at the youth events, sport climbing then made its debut at the Tokyo 2020 Games, joining the Olympic program as a new sport. Janja Garnbret representing Slovenia and Alberto Ginés López of Spain made history as the inaugural women's and men's climbing combined Olympic champions.

SURFING

Surfing in the 2024 Olympics is scheduled to take place over five days within a 10-day window, depending on weather conditions, spanning from July 27 to August 8. If conditions permit, both titles will be awarded on Tuesday, July 30.

The venue for these events is the legendary surfing spot, Teahupo'o reef pass in Tahiti, French Polynesia, setting a record for the farthest medal competition stage outside the host city.

Surfers execute maneuvers and tricks on a wave, which are evaluated by five judges according to the variety, type, and difficulty of the maneuvers. Additionally, judges assess surfers based on their speed, power, and flow, which refers to the seamless connection between consecutive moves. Shortboards are the preferred surfboards for the Olympics because they are smaller, faster and more maneuverable than longboards, making them ideal for executing impressive tricks.

The idyllic setting of crystal-clear waters and tropical vegetation is famous for its wave, among the most impressive in the world, towering up to two, three, and even seven meters in height. But it's the swell that breaks over the shallow reefs of Tahiti, French Polynesia that athletes fear the most. With a succession of moves, speed, power, and flow, the spectacle is poised to be an outstanding one.

A total of 48 surfers, divided equally, will compete in the shortboard events, vying for **two Olympic titles**:
- men's finals on Tuesday, July 30 at 15:34 Tahiti time
- women's finals on Tuesday, July 30 at 16:15 Tahiti time

Surfing originated in Polynesia, particularly in places like Hawaii, Tahiti, and Samoa, where it was an integral part of the culture. Early Polynesians rode waves on wooden boards, with surfing playing an important role in their society. In the late 18th century, European explorers documented surfing, leading to its spread beyond the Pacific. In the early 20th century, surfing experienced a revival with Duke Kahanamoku, an Olympic swimmer and one of the best surfers on the Hawaiian Islands, popularizing the sport both locally and internationally. Throughout the 20th century, surfing evolved alongside technological advancements in board design and became increasingly associated with beach culture.

In the 1920s, supporters of surfing, including native Hawaiian Duke Kahanamoku, a three-time Olympic swimming freestyle champion, began campaigning for the sport to be added to the Olympic program. Nearly a century later, surfing finally made it onto the Olympic program for the Tokyo 2020 Games. The inaugural champions were Carissa Moore from the USA in the women's discipline and Brazil's Ítalo Ferreira in the men's event.

SWIMMING

At the Olympic Games, swimming contests are held in a 50-meter long pool. The four strokes of Olympic swimming – for both individual and relay races – are freestyle, breaststroke, backstroke, and butterfly.

Freestyle
Freestyle is a category of swimming competition where athletes are permitted to utilize any swim technique, offering the flexibility to adopt the stroke that best suits their individual strengths and preferences. The *front crawl* is often preferred for its efficiency and speed, which is why it's commonly associated with the term *freestyle stroke*. These races are the most common, with distances ranging from 50 meters (55 yards) to 1,500 meters (1,600 yards), also known as the mile.

Breaststroke
Breaststroke is a swimming style in which the athlete is on their chest and the torso does not rotate. It is the most popular choice for recreational swimmers due to the extended periods with the head above water, and it can be swum comfortably at slow speeds. Typically, beginners in swimming classes start with either breaststroke or crawl. Nevertheless, at the competitive level, swimming breaststroke at speed requires endurance and strength comparable to other techniques. Sometimes is called the *frog* stroke, as the movements of arms and legs resemble those of a frog swimming. It is the slowest of any competitive techniques and is believed to be the oldest style of swimming.

Backstroke
Backstroke or back crawl is the only one of these styles swum on the back. This type offers the benefit of easy breathing, yet presents the drawback of swimmers lacking visibility of their direction. Additionally, backstroke features a distinct start compared to the other three competitive types: it starts in the water, while the others start from the blocks. The swimming style is similar to an upside down front crawl.

Both backstroke and front crawl are categorized as long-axis strokes, while the other two, breaststroke and butterfly, are considered short-axis. While long-axis types rotate along a horizontal axis from head to toe, short-axis styles have a hinge like motion that originates from the core and hips.

Butterfly
The butterfly is a stroke swum on the chest, with both arms moving symmetrically, accompanied by the butterfly kick (also known as the *dolphin kick*) along with the movement of the hips and chest. In the early 1930s, a variant of the breaststroke emerged, which eventually evolved into the butterfly style. By 1952, the decision to distinguish between the butterfly and breaststroke styles became logical. As a result, in 1953, the breaststroke was split into two distinct events. Furthermore, while traditional breaststroke required the whip kick, the new butterfly stroke allowed the use of butterfly kick. The difference lies in the fact that the whip kick involves an outward and backward motion of both legs, (much like a frog), whereas the butterfly kick involves a simultaneous undulating motion of both legs, resembling the movement of a dolphin's tail.

There is also the mixed medley that involves all four strokes, with swimmers switching between them. The distances also vary, with different skills needed for a 50-meter race to a 1500 meters. Explosiveness, endurance, strength, and technique are all essential qualities for swimmers.

Swimming races in 2024 will take place at the Paris La Défense Arena, featuring a total of **35 medal events** over the course of nine days (17 for women, 17 for men, and 1 mixed event).

Finals contested on Saturday, 27th of July
- men's 400 m freestyle at 20:42
- women's 400 m freestyle at 20:55
- women's 4 × 100 m freestyle relay at 21:37
- men's 4 × 100 m freestyle relay at 21:50

Finals contested on Sunday, 28th of July
- men's 400 m individual medley at 20:30
- women's 100 m butterfly at 20:45
- men's 100 m breaststroke at 21:54

Finals contested on Monday, 29th of July
- women's 400 m individual medley at 20:30
- men's 200 m freestyle at 20:43
- men's 100 m backstroke at 21:22
- women's 100 m breaststroke at 21:32
- women's 200 m freestyle at 21:48

Finals contested on Tuesday, 30th of July
- women's 100 m backstroke at 20:57
- men's 800 m freestyle at 21:03
- men's 4 × 200 m freestyle relay at 21:59

Finals contested on Wednesday, 31st of July
- women's 100 m freestyle at 20:30
- men's 200 m butterfly at 20:36
- women's 1500 m freestyle at 21:04
- men's 200 m breaststroke at 22:08
- men's 100 m freestyle at 22:15

Finals contested on Thursday, 1st of August
- women's 200 m butterfly at 20:30
- men's 200 m backstroke at 20:37
- women's 200 m breaststroke at 21:03
- women's 4 × 200 m freestyle relay at 21:48

Finals contested on Friday, 2nd of August
- men's 50 m freestyle at 20:30
- women's 200 m backstroke at 20:39
- men's 200 m individual medley at 20:49

Finals contested on Saturday, 3rd of August
- men's 100 m butterfly at 20:30
- women's 200 m individual medley at 20:59
- women's 800 m freestyle at 21:09
- mixed 4 × 100 m medley relay at 21:33

Finals contested on Sunday, 4th of August
- women's 50 m freestyle at 18:30
- men's 1500 m freestyle at 18:36
- men's 4 × 100 m medley relay at 19:12
- women's 4 × 100 m medley relay at 19:35

Swimming has its origins in prehistoric times, but it wasn't until the 19th century that it evolved into a competitive sport. Its emergence as a recreational activity occurred in the 1830s in England. By 1837, the National Swimming Society of Great Britain was holding regular swimming competitions in six artificial swimming pools, built around London. Initially, most swimmers used the breaststroke, or a form of it. Over time, a wider variety of strokes were later added to the competitions and now feature at the Games.

Swimming has been a staple of every modern Summer Olympics. While the initial Olympic races took place in natural environments—with swimmers competing in the Bay of Zea in 1896 Athens, starting from the 1908 Games in London, the events have been conducted in pools.

The inaugural Games in 1896 featured only freestyle events. The backstroke competition was introduced at the 1900 Paris Olympics. The 1904 St. Louis Games marked the debut of a separate breaststroke race. The butterfly stroke made its first appearance at the 1956 Melbourne Games. Women's swimming was added to the Olympic program during the 1912 Games in Stockholm, which featured two races. Today, the swimming events for both men and women at the Olympic Games are identical.

The 1924 Olympics were the first to use of the standard 50-meter pool with marked lanes. Initially, in freestyle events, swimmers would dive from the pool walls, with blocks being introduced for the first time at the 1936 Games. The flip-turn technique was developed by the 1950s, refining swimming efficiency. In 1976 Montreal Olympics, goggles were permitted for the first time, providing swimmers with enhanced vision and comfort.

Over the years, there has been a consistent decrease in swimming times, attributed to improved training techniques and advancements within the sport. Male swimmers wore full-body swimsuits until the 1940s, which created more drag in the water compared to modern swimwear. Additionally, pool designs have evolved to minimize drag. Various features such as proper pool depth, wave and current elimination, increased lane width, energy-absorbing racing lane lines and gutters, as well as innovative hydraulic, acoustic, illumination, and swimwear designs, contribute to reducing swimming resistance and enhancing pool speed.

Olympic swimming has been dominated by athletes representing the United States, who have won a total of 579 medals, conquering 257 golds, followed by Australia, with 212 medals, including 69 golds.

Among the swimming greats, USA's Michael Phelps, stands out as the most successful and decorated Olympian of all time, with an impressive haul of 28 medals. Phelps also holds the record for the most Olympic gold medals of all time, with an astounding 23 golds to his name.

TABLE TENNIS

The table tennis tournaments at the 2024 Olympics will be held between July 27 and August 10 at the South Paris Arena 4, part of the Paris Expo Porte de Versailles.

Table tennis, also known as ping-pong, is a racket sport derived from tennis played on a table divided into two halves by a net. Players, either individually or in teams of two, take turns returning a light, hollow ball over the net onto the opposing half using small rackets or "paddles" comprising a wooden blade coated with a rubber surface on both sides. Ping pong play is fast, requiring a high level of physical skill, agility, and hand-eye coordination. Players must possess quick reflexes, precise ball control, and the ability to move swiftly around the table to return shots effectively. The fast-paced nature of the sport demands excellent motor skills and physical fitness. The game is characterized by an emphasis on spin relative to other ball sports, which can heavily affect the ball's trajectory.

Singles matches are a best-of-seven games format, with the first player to 11 points (by a margin of two clear points) winning each game. Team matches consist of four singles matches and one doubles match, each played in a best-of-five games format. Each team comprises three players and matches end when a team has won three individual games. In doubles matches, players take turns to hit the ball.

Due to its small playing area, suitability for indoor play in all weather conditions and the relative accessibility of equipment, table tennis is enjoyed worldwide not just as a competitive sport, but also as a recreational activity for players of all skill levels and ages.

A total of 172 table tennis players will compete across **five medal events**:
- mixed doubles finals on Tuesday, July 30 at 14:30
- women's singles finals on Saturday, August 3 at 14:30
- men's singles finals on Sunday, August 4 at 14:30
- men's team finals on Friday, August 9 at 15:00
- women's team finals on Saturday, August 10 at 15:00

Table tennis is derived from lawn tennis and was initially played as post-dinner entertainment among upper-class English families, who improvised equipment from whatever was available. They would use books as a net, cigar box lids or other books as rackets and a golf-ball or a rounded-off bottle cork as the ball. Fortunately, table tennis equipment has evolved over time and in 1926 the first world championships were held in London. Widely embraced in Asia, table tennis is played by over 40 million people around the globe, making it one of the most popular sports worldwide.

Table tennis made its Olympic debut at the Seoul Games in 1988, featuring singles and doubles tournaments for women and men. In 2008, the doubles competition was replaced by the team event and the program expanded further for the 2020 Tokyo Games to include mixed doubles.

Since its introduction to the Olympic program in 1988, athletes representing China have dominated table tennis, securing 32 out of the total 37 gold medals awarded and amassing a total of 60 medals out of the 115 awarded thus far at the Games.

TAEKWONDO

Taekwondo is a Korean martial art characterized by its emphasis on kicking techniques, particularly high kicks. It combines elements of self-defense, combat sport, exercise, and philosophy. Taekwondo training typically includes various forms of sparring, patterns (known as *poomsae* or *kata*), breaking techniques, and conditioning drills. Its philosophy emphasizes discipline, respect, and self-control, aiming to cultivate both physical and mental strength in practitioners. Taekwondo athletes wear a uniform, known as *dobok*, which serves as both a functional outfit for training and competitions, and embodies symbolic importance within the martial art, representing discipline, respect, and tradition.

The aim of taekwondo is for an athlete to kick and punch their opponent while evading incoming strikes. The trademark of this martial art is its combination of kicking and punching movements in quick succession. Matches are fought on an octagonal mat for three rounds of two minutes each. Points are awarded according to the degree of difficulty of techniques used; for example, a kick to the head scores higher than punches and kicks to the trunk. Spinning kicks are also rewarded with extra points. Penalties may be given to athletes for various faults.

At the Olympics, each weight class will feature 16 athletes in the bracket. The competition starts with the first round and proceeds to the quarterfinals, semifinals, and final. For the most part, the tournament is single elimination, with one key exception: any athlete who loses to one of the two finalists gets pulled into the repechage for a chance at winning a bronze medal.

Each of the two finalists will have defeated three athletes en route to the gold medal match: one in the first round, one in the quarterfinals, and one in the semifinals. The athletes who lost in the first round and quarterfinals will face each other in a repechage match. The winner of this advances to a bronze medal match against the athlete who lost in the semifinals. This process happens for both finalists, so there will be two separate bronze medal matches and therefore two bronze medals awarded.

Taekwondo cultivates not only the development of physical skills, but also character traits such as discipline, respect, and perseverance, which are valuable both on and off the mat.

A total of 128 taekwondo fighters, with an equal distribution between men and women, will compete at the Grand Palais across **eight medal events**:
- women's 49 kg finals on Wednesday, August 7 at 21:23
- men's 58 kg finals on Wednesday, August 7 at 21:39
- men's 68 kg finals on Thursday, August 8 at 21:23
- women's 57 kg finals on Thursday, August 8 at 21:39
- women's 67 kg finals on Friday, August 9 at 21:23
- men's 80 kg finals on Friday, August 9 at 21:39
- men's +80 kg finals on Saturday, August 10 at 21:23
- women +67 kg finals on Saturday, August 10 at 21:39

Taekwondo, which translates to "the art of kicking and punching", is a martial art with roots dating back to the Three Kingdoms Period of Ancient Korea (c. 57 BC to 668 AD) when Silla Dynasty warriors began to develop a martial art known as *taekkyon* ("foot-hand"). The modern form of taekwondo was developed during the 1940s and 1950s by Korean martial artists and is influenced by indigenous fighting styles, as well as Chinese martial arts. After Korea was liberated from Japanese occupation in 1945, there was a movement to revive and promote Korean culture, including martial arts. Various schools and organizations emerged, each with its own approach to training and techniques. In 1955, several of these schools came together to establish a unified martial art, which they named "taekwondo". The sport then went international and in 1973 the first taekwondo world championships were held in Seoul.

Taekwondo's first Olympic appearance came at the Seoul 1988 Games, when it was contested as a demonstration event. It appeared again as a demonstration sport at the Barcelona Games in 1992, but was absent from the Olympic program at Atlanta 1996. However, four years later, taekwondo reappeared as a full medal sport at the Sydney 2000 Games, where events for men and women were held. It has been a part of the Olympic program ever since.

Before the 2012 Summer Olympics, nations were limited to sending a maximum of two male and two female competitors, regardless of whether they were the host nation or not. Starting from the 2016 Summer Olympics, this restriction was removed, allowing each nation to qualify one athlete per weight category.

While taekwondo competitions were previously dominated by athletes from South Korea (they lead the medal table with a total of 22, including 12 gold), this is no longer the case. For example, at London 2012, gold medals were awarded to athletes from eight different nations, highlighting the increasing popularity and competitiveness within the sport.

Some nations have even made history by winning their first Olympic medals through taekwondo—including Vietnam in 2000, Afghanistan in 2008, Gabon in 2012, and Niger and Jordan in 2016—or their first-ever female Olympic medals, including Iran and Côte d'Ivoire, also in 2016.

TENNIS

The tennis tournaments at the 2024 Games in Paris are scheduled to take place from July 27 to August 4 at the iconic Roland Garros venue, on a clay court surface.

Tennis is a racket sport that is played either individually against a single opponent (singles) or between two teams of two players each (doubles) on a rectangular court with a net in the center. Each player uses a tennis racket that is strung with cord to strike a hollow rubber ball covered with felt back and forth over the net (or even around it), aiming to land it within the boundaries of the opponent's side of the court. The objective is to score points by successfully hitting the ball in such a way that the opponent is unable to return it within the prescribed boundaries. The player who is unable to return the ball validly will not gain a point, while the opposite player will.

A tennis match is composed of points, games, and sets. A set is made up of a minimum of six games, each of which consists of points. To win a set, a side must secure six games with a lead of at least two games over the opponent. If the set is tied at six games each, a tie-break is played to decide the set winner. A match is won when a player or a doubles team has won the majority of the required number of sets. Matches are conducted using either a best-of-three (first to two sets wins) or best-of-five (first to three sets wins) set format. The best-of-five set format is currently only used in men's singles matches at Grand Slam tournaments.

Tennis is notable for its versatility, as it can be played on a variety of surfaces both outdoors and indoors. It is commonly played on grass, clay, and hardcourts made of concrete or asphalt topped with acrylic. Indoor play occasionally utilizes carpet or historically, hardwood flooring. Artificial turf courts are also available.

The Olympic tennis tournament features a classic single-elimination format, with 64 players participating in both the men's and women's singles draws. The doubles draw includes 32 teams for both women and men, while the mixed doubles draw consists of 16 mixed teams. In the single-elimination format, the winning team or player progresses to the next round, while the losing team or player is eliminated. This continues until the semifinals, where losing semifinalists are not eliminated but instead compete in a bronze medal match. The winning semifinalists, of course, will contest the gold medal match.

Singles matches are played in a best-of-three sets format, with a tiebreak in the final set decided by the first player to reach seven points, in contrast to the 10-point tiebreak used in Grand Slam final sets. Doubles matches also follow a best-of-three sets format, with a match tiebreak to ten points replacing a final set.

The 2024 Olympic tournament marks the return of clay court tennis to the Summer Games for the first time since Barcelona 1992. Rafael Nadal and Novak Djokovic are expected to compete, alongside favorites Carlos Alcaraz, Jannik Sinner, and Alexander Zverev in the men's singles draw. Iga Swiatek is the heavy favorite to win the women singles competition.

A total of 172 players will compete across **five medal events**:
- mixed doubles finals on Friday, August 2 at 19:00
- women's singles finals on Saturday, August 3 at 14:00
- men's doubles finals on Saturday, August 3 at 16:00
- men's singles finals on Sunday, August 4 at 14:00
- women's doubles finals on Sunday, August 4 at 16:00

The precursor to tennis, known as "jeu de paume" or "game of the hand," originated in France during the 11th century. This early form of the game was played in monastery courtyards, where players used their palms to strike a ball against walls and sloping roofs. It wasn't until the 16th century that rackets came into use and the game began to be called tennis. The term is derived from the French word *tenez*, meaning "receive!" or "take!"—an interjection used by the server to his opponent. By this time, it had gained popularity among European nobility, leading to the construction of indoor courts known as "tennis courts" in palaces and estates.

The modern version of tennis as we know it today began to take shape in 19th-century England. With the sport's rising popularity surpassing that of croquet, the All England Croquet Club allowed its lawns to be used for tennis. The first tennis championships were held in England in the late 19th century and the sport's popularity continued to grow, leading to the establishment of international tournaments and federations.

The rules of modern tennis have remained largely unchanged since the 1890s. There have been two notable exceptions: until 1961, the server was required to keep one foot on the ground at all times and the tiebreak system was introduced in the 1970s. A more recent addition to professional tennis is the implementation of electronic review technology, combined with a point-challenge system, which enables players to challenge line calls using a system known as Hawk-Eye.

The most important tournaments are the four Grand Slams (also referred to as the majors): the Australian Open in Melbourne, played on hardcourts; the French Open in Roland Garros – Paris, played on red clay courts; Wimbledon in London, played on grass courts; and the US Open in New York, also played on hardcourts.

Tennis made its debut at the first modern Olympiad in Athens in 1896, but was withdrawn from the program after the 1924 Olympic Games due to disagreements over the definition of amateur players. After two appearances as a demonstration sport in 1968 and 1984 (with a U-21 age limit), it was reinstated as a full medal sport at the 1988 Olympic Games in Seoul. Since then, tennis has been a permanent fixture at every Summer Games, open to all players, regardless of age and status.

The playing surface from 1988 has been hardcourt, with the exceptions of the 1992 Olympics, which featured a clay court, and the 2012 Olympics, played on a grass court. The changing playing surface gives certain players different advantages and disadvantages not seen in most other Olympic sports.

Some of the world's greatest players have competed in recent years. Among them, several superstars have clinched the gold medal, including Andre Agassi who secured the singles Olympic title in 1996; Rafael Nadal, Olympic champion in the singles event in 2008 and doubles in 2016; Andy Murray, who claimed the singles Olympic crown in both 2012 and 2016; Stan Wawrinka and Roger Federer won the Olympic doubles title in 2008; and Serena and Venus Williams who have won eight Olympic titles between them. Venus Williams clinched the singles Olympic title in 2000, while Serena Williams captured the same title in 2012. Together, they also secured three doubles Olympic titles in 2000, 2008, and 2012.

The current singles champions are Belinda Bencic from Switzerland and Alexander Zverev from Germany in the women's and men's events, respectively, at the Tokyo Olympics.

TRACK & FIELD / ATHLETICS

Track and field or athletics events at the 2024 Olympics in Paris are scheduled to run between August 1 to 11. This sport serve as the backbone of the Summer Games.

The term "athletics" traces its roots back to the ancient Greek *athlētēs*, meaning "combatant in public games". Initially, the term described athletic contests in general like sporting competition based primarily on human physical feats. However, in the 19th century, its meaning narrowed in Europe to describe sports involving competitive running, walking, jumping, and throwing, a definition prominent in the United Kingdom and British language.

In much of North America, athletics is synonymous with sports in general, retaining its historical usage. The word "athletics" is rarely used to refer to the sport of athletics in this region. Track and field is used in the United States to refer to athletics events, including race walking and marathon running, though they are generally designated as athletics elsewhere.

Modern athletics, or track and field, is composed of various running, jumping, throwing, walking, and combined events. Due to its many categories and disciplines, track and field involves the most participants in a single sport at the Olympic Games.

The **track** program at the Olympics includes sprints, middle-distance and long-distance events, along with hurdles, steeplechase races and relays, for both women and men. These competitions take place on the 400-meter oval track within the Olympic stadium, consisting of two straight sections and two curved bends.

Sprints

Races over short distances, or sprints, are among the oldest running competitions. The first thirteen editions of the ancient Olympic Games featured only one event, the *stadion* race, which was a race from one end of the stadium to the other. These kind of events focus on athletes reaching and maintaining their highest possible running speed. Three sprinting races are held at the Olympics: the 100, 200, and 400 meters.

Originally all runners started from a standing position, but in the 1880s the crouch start was invented, and it became a rule that athletes must start with both feet and both hands on the track. Sprinters initiate the race in the crouched position in the starting blocks, then lean forward and gradually transition to an upright position as the race progresses and momentum builds. Throughout all sprinting events, athletes remain in their designated lane on the track. The 100 meters race primarily focus on acceleration to reach the athlete's maximum speed. Beyond this distance, all sprints increasingly incorporate an element of endurance.

Men's sprint races were part of the first modern Olympic Games in Athens in 1896, featuring the 100 and 400 meters. The 200 meters was introduced in the second edition of the Olympics in 1900. Only men were permitted to compete until the 1928 Games in Amsterdam, where the use of a 400-meter track became the standard for track and field. As mentioned above, women's participation began in 1928 with the 100 meters, followed by the women's 200 at the 1948 Games and the women's 400 at the 1964 Games.

Technology has continuously enhanced sprint performances, such as the introduction of starting blocks, synthetic track materials and advancements in shoe equipment. In 1924, athletes used a small shovel to dig holes for the start of the race. The world record for the 100-meter dash was 10.4 seconds in 1924, which decreased to 10.2 seconds in 1948 with the introduction of starting blocks. The relentless pursuit of faster athletes combined with improved technology has reduced the men's world record to 9.58 seconds in less than 100 years.

Middle-distance

The middle-distance track events comprise the 800 and 1500 meters. Both men's races have been integral parts of the Olympic schedule since 1896. The women's 800 meters event made its debut in 1928, marking the first distance running event for women. It wasn't included again until 1960, after which it became a permanent fixture. The women's 1500-meter race was added to the Olympics for the first time in the 1972 Games.

Middle distance events can begin in one of two ways: a staggered or a waterfall start. In the 800-meter race, athletes begin in individual lanes staggered before the turn. They must stay in their lanes for the first 100 meters before cutting in to run as a pack. This rule was introduced to reduce jostling between runners in the early stages of the race. The 1500-meter and also longer events typically use a waterfall start, where runners begin the race from a standing position along a curved starting line and then immediately cut in towards the innermost track to follow the shortest route to the finish.

Beyond the short distances of sprinting events, factors such as an athlete's reactions and top speed becomes less important, while qualities such as pace, tactics, and endurance become more so.

Long-distance

In track and field competitions, there are two long-distance running events: the 5000 and the 10,000 meters. These races trace their historical roots back to the 3-mile and 6-mile contests. Both men's races made their Olympic debut at the 1912 Stockholm Games. Initially, the women's long-distance event was the 3000 meters, included in the Olympic program in 1984, but it was later replaced by the 5000 race in 1996. The women's 10,000 meters premiered at the 1988 Games.

In terms of competition rules and physical demands, long-distance track races have much in common with middle-distance events, except that pacing, stamina, and tactics become much greater factors in performances. The longer the run, the less likely the burst of speed known as the "finishing kick" at the end of the race.

Marathons, although also long-distance events, typically take place on street courses and are conducted separately from other track and field contests.

Relay races

Relay races stand out as the only track and field event in which teams of athletes engage in direct competition with one another. A team comprises four runners, each completing their assigned distance, known as a leg, before passing a baton to a teammate to begin their section. There is a designated zone where athletes must perform the exchange. Teams risk disqualification if they fail to complete the handover within this area or if the baton is dropped during the race. Deliberate obstruction of other competitors can also lead to disqualification.

Relay events emerged in the United States during the 1880s as a variation of charity races among firemen, who would pass a red pennant to teammates every 300 yards. At the Olympics, two relay events are contested: the 4×100 and the 4×400 meters. Both men's races were introduced at the 1912 Games, following a one-off medley relay featured in the 1908 Olympics. The women's 4×100 meters debuted in the 1928 Games, while the women's 4×400 was added in 1972. The first Olympic 4×400 meters mixed relay took place at the 2020 Games.

The 4×100 meters event is run strictly within the same lane, meaning that the team collectively completes one circuit of the track. In the 4×400 event, teams remain in their lanes until the second leg runner passes the first bend, after which they can move towards the inner part of the track. During the second and third baton exchanges, runners position themselves according to their standing, with leading teams taking the inner lanes and the slower ones waiting in the outer lanes for the exchange.

Speed is essential in both events, and the ability to pass the baton is crucial in the shorter one, where each runner covers 100 meters. Exchanging while sprinting at about 25 miles per hour adds an element of suspense to the event. Many races have been won or lost by the quality of baton passing.

Hurdling and steeplechase

The hurdling events combine sprinting with negotiating a series of obstacles known as hurdles. The popularity of these races featuring obstacles grew in 19th century England. The earliest known event, held in 1830, was a variation of the 100-yard dash incorporating heavy wooden barriers as obstacles. In 1864, a competition between the Oxford and Cambridge Athletic Clubs refined this concept, introducing a 120-yard race with ten hurdles standing at 3 feet 6 inches in height (1.06 meters). French organizers later adopted this race into the metric system (adding 28 centimeters), and the basics of the 110 meters hurdles race have remained largely unchanged throughout the years. The origin of the 400 meters can also be traced back to Oxford, where around 1860, a competition was held over 440 yards with twelve 1.06-meter-high wooden barriers placed along the course. Modern regulations for the event emerged from the 1900 Olympics, fixing the distance at 400 meters and positioning ten 91 centimeters (3 ft) hurdles 35 meters apart on the track. The women's hurdles are slightly lower, set at 84 centimeters (2 ft 9 in) for the 100-meter event and 76 centimeters (2 ft 6 in) for the 400-meter race.

The 110 meters hurdles has featured in every modern Olympics, while the 400 was introduced in the second edition of the Games. Women initially competed in the 80 meters hurdles event, added to the Olympic program in 1932. It was extended to 100 at the 1972 Games, while the women's 400-meter event debuted at the Olympics in 1984.

Athletes may knock down hurdles during their race, but they face disqualification if they run outside their designated lane or use their hands to knock them over. The goal is to make the hurdling action smooth and rhythmic without disrupting forward progress.

Outside of hurdling contests, steeplechase races are another track and field event featuring obstacles. This discipline, like hurdling, is derived from student competitions in Oxford, England, but it was originally a human variation of steeplechase horse racing. Such an event was held on a track for the 1879 English championships, and the 1900 Olympics featured men's 2500 and 4000 meters steeplechase races. The event was contested over various distances until the 1920 Games established the 3000 meters as the regular distance. The race's standards were set in 1954, and it is held on a 400-meter circuit featuring seven water jumps (one per lap) and 28 hurdles. Despite the long history of men's steeplechase in track and field, women's events first appeared at the Olympics in 2008.

The **field** disciplines are contested on, within, and around the track in the Olympic stadium, in the jumping area (high jump and pole vault), the jumping pit (long jump and triple jump), the throwing circle (shot put, discus, and hammer throw), and the javelin runway. Athletes compete one after the other, with each event including a qualifying stage where they earn their spot in the final.

Long jump

The long jump is one of the oldest track and field events, tracing its roots back to the ancient Greek pentathlon contest. In this event, athletes would execute a short run-up and jump into an area while holding small weights, *halteres*, in each hand. They would swing these weights back and drop them near the end of the jump to gain extra momentum and distance. Although no weights are used in the modern long jump, which was standardized in England and the United States around 1860, it bears resemblance to its ancient counterpart.

Athletes in the modern event sprint along a section of track leading to a jumping board and a sandpit. The leap must be executed before a marked line, with the distance achieved measured from the nearest point of sand disturbed by the athlete's body. The inaugural Olympics in 1896 included a men's long jump competition, while a women's event was introduced at the 1948 Games. A standing long jump contest, where athletes leap from a static position without a run-up, was part of the men's Olympic program from 1900 to 1912.

Professional long jumpers possess strong acceleration and sprinting abilities, as speed is paramount for a successful jump. Athletes approach the runway at nearly top speed, plant a foot on the takeoff board, and launch into the air. A legal try requires that no part of the forward foot extend beyond the board.

Triple jump

Similar to the previous event, the triple jump takes place on a track leading to a sandpit. Originally, athletes would hop on the same leg twice before jumping into the pit, but this was replaced by the current "hop, step, and jump" sequence from 1900 onward. The athlete approaches the runway and launches off a board, similar in style, but slightly slower than long jumpers. The first segment involves the athlete executing a hop by landing on the same foot from which they took off. Next, they take a step, landing on the other foot, and conclude with a jump into the sandpit.

The men's triple jump competition has been a constant feature at the modern Games, but it wasn't until 1996 that a women's version gained Olympic status. The men's standing triple jump event was part of the Olympics in 1900 and 1904, but such competitions have since become very uncommon.

High jump

The aim of high jumping is to clear a thin bar positioned atop two standards, with athletes staying in the competition as long as they avoid three consecutive misses. Competitors can enter at any height above the minimum and have the option to pass heights as the bar is raised.

The earliest recorded high jumping competitions date back to Scotland in the 19th century, with further contests organized in England in 1840. By 1865, the fundamental rules of the modern event were standardized there. Athletes execute a short run-up before taking off from one foot to clear the horizontal bar, landing on a cushioned area. The men's high jump debuted at the 1896 Olympics, followed by a women's competition in 1928. The standing high jump was contested at the Games from 1900 to 1912, but is now uncommon outside of its use as an exercise drill.

Historically, jumping technique has played a significant role in the event's evolution. In the late 19th century, high jumpers typically cleared the bar feet first, but the straddle technique became prominent in the mid-20th century. In this method, the athlete approached the bar head-on and cleared it by lifting their body over it while facing downwards, with the legs straddling the bar. This allowed for more efficient clearance of higher heights and became the dominant technique for several decades.

Dick Fosbury revolutionized the sport in the late 1960s by pioneering the "Fosbury flop", which won him the gold at the 1968 Olympics. Fosbury approached the bar diagonally and cleared it by arching his back and flipping over headfirst, with his body facing upwards. This method enabled greater clearance heights and became the standard from the 1980s onward.

Pole vault

Pole vaulters attempt to clear a crossbar positioned on uprights, landing in an inflated or composition pit. Competitors can enter at any height above the minimum and can choose to pass heights as the bar is raised. They remain in the event as long as they avoid three consecutive misses.

The use of poles for vaulting distances was recorded in Fierljeppen contests in the Frisian area of Europe, while vaulting for height was seen at gymnastics competitions in Germany in the 1770s. One of the earliest recorded pole vault competitions occurred in Cumbria, England in 1843. The basic rules and techniques of the event originated in the United States, with regulations prohibiting athletes from moving their hands along the pole. Bamboo poles were introduced in the 20th century, along with a metal box in the runway for planting them. Landing mattresses were introduced in the mid-20th century to protect vaulters clearing increasingly greater heights.

In the modern event, athletes sprint down a strip of track, plant the pole in the metal box, leave the ground, and pull themselves upward until they are almost in a handstand position on the pole. As they near the crossbar, they twist, let go of the pole, arch over the bar feet first and face down, and then fall backward onto the landing mattress.

While earlier versions used wooden, metal or bamboo, modern poles are generally made from artificial materials such as fiberglass or carbon fiber. The pole vault has been an Olympic event for men since 1896, but it wasn't until over a century later, in 2000, that the first women's Olympic competition took place.

Shot put

The putting action is best described as shoving the shot, as the rules prohibit the arm from extending behind the shoulders during the putting motion. The shot, a spherical object, is made of metal.

Its origins can be traced back to prehistoric times, with contests involving rocks. During the Middle Ages, stone put competitions were known in Scotland and the *steinstossen* was recorded in Switzerland. In the 17th century, cannonball throwing contests within the English military served as a precursor to the modern sport. The term "shot" derives from the use of round shot-style ammunition in these competitions. The modern rules were first laid out in 1860 and required that competitors execute legal throws within a square zone measuring seven feet on each side. This was later modified to a circular area with a diameter of seven feet (2.135 meters) in 1906, with the shot's weight standardized to 16 pounds (7.26 kilograms).

It became an Olympic sport for men since 1896, with a women's competition using an 8.82 pounds (4 kilograms) shot added in 1948. Further throwing techniques have arisen since the post-war era as athletes must gather momentum for the put by rapid twisting movements. In the 1950s, Parry O'Brien popularized the 180-degree turn and throw technique, commonly known as the "glide", breaking the world record 17 times along the way and winning three Olympic medals (two gold). Aleksandr Baryshnikov and Brian Oldfield introduced the "spin" or rotational technique in 1976, where the putter spins one and a half turns before releasing the shot.

Discus throw

In the discus throw, competitors strive to hurl a heavy disc as far as possible. The athlete, positioned in a designated circular arc, launches it after completing one and a half body rotations. They take turns in a series of throws, with the best effort determining the winner.

As one of the events within the ancient Greek pentathlon, the history of the discus throw dates back to 708 BC. In ancient times, a heavy circular disc was hurled from a fixed standing position on a small pedestal, a style that was revived for the 1896 Olympics.

By the 1912 Games, the ancient standing throw had been replaced by contests starting within a 2.5-meter (8.2-foot) squared area. The discus implement was standardized to 2 kilograms (4.4 pounds) in weight and 22 centimeters (8 inches) in diameter in 1907. For women, it weighs 1 kilogram (2.2 pounds). Discus throw was among the first women's disciplines introduced at the Olympics in 1928.

The first modern athlete to throw the discus while rotating the whole body was Czech athlete František Janda-Suk. He developed the technique when studying the position of the famous statue of Discobolus and won the Olympic silver medal in 1900.

Javelin throw

The javelin throw, originally utilized for warfare and hunting, has its roots in prehistoric times. Alongside the discus, it was the second throwing event in the ancient Olympic pentathlon. In the late 19th century, the javelin throw gained considerable popularity in Scandinavia, with athletes from the region remaining among the most dominant throwers in men's competitions.

In the modern event, contestants execute a short run-up on a track, aiming to achieve maximum distance with their throw. To ensure a legal try, the athlete must release the javelin behind the foul line and maintain his foot within the throwing zone. The runway measures a minimum of 30 meters in length and is covered with the same surface as the track. A valid throw mandates that the javelin lands point-first, though it is not necessary for it to stick.

The first Olympic men's contest was held in 1908, with a women's competition introduced in 1932. The first javelins were made of various types of wood, but in the 1950s, former athlete Bud Held introduced a hollow, then a metal javelin, both of which increased throwers performances. Another former athlete, Miklós Németh invented the rough-tailed javelin and throws reached in excess of 100 meters – edging towards the limits of the stadium.

Concerns over safety led to a redesign of the men's event in 1991 to reduce distances and allow for easier measurement. Rough-tailed designs were banned and distances achieved with such javelins were removed from the record books. The women's event underwent a similar redesign in 1999. The current javelin specifications are 2.6 to 2.7 meters and weights of 800 grams for men, and 2.2 to 2.3 meters and weights of 600 grams for women.

Hammer throw

The earliest documented precursors to the modern hammer throw originate from the Tailteann Games of ancient Ireland. These games featured activities like throwing either a weight attached to a rope, a large rock on a wooden handle, or even tossing a chariot wheel on a wooden axle. Other ancient contests included launching a cast iron ball attached to a wooden handle, which laid the groundwork for the term "hammer throw" due to their resemblance to the tools. In 16th century England, there were recorded competitions involving the hurling of genuine blacksmith's sledgehammers.

The hammer implement was standardized in 1887, marking the beginning of competitions that closely resemble the modern event. The throwing circle is slightly smaller than that of the discus, 2.135 meters in diameter compared to 2.5 meters. The weight, which is not a conventional hammer, but rather a metal ball, was set at 16 pounds (7.26 kilograms), while the attached wire had to measure between 1.175 meters and 1.215 meters. The thrower grips the handle at the end of the wire opposite from the ball and releases it after completing three or four body turns to generate maximum centrifugal force.

The men's hammer throw debuted as an Olympic event in 1900, whereas the women's event—using an 8.82 pounds (4-kilogram) weight—was not contested until much later, finally appearing at the Games in 2000.

The distances achieved by male athletes increased significantly from the 1950s onward due to improved equipment using denser metals, a switch to concrete throwing areas, and the adoption of more sophisticated training techniques. Historically, professional hammer throwers were typically large, robust individuals. However, qualities such as refined technique, speed, and flexibility have become increasingly important in the modern era as the legal throwing area has been reduced from 90 to 34.92 degrees and the throwing technique involves three to four controlled rotations.

The Olympic program also features two combined disciplines: the seven-event women's heptathlon and the ten-event men's decathlon. The ancient Olympic pentathlon, which included long jump, javelin, discus, the *stadion* race and wrestling, served as a precursor to the track and field combined events. These contests test athletes' abilities across a range of disciplines, with the most versatile competitor earning the gold medal.

The women's heptathlon and men's decathlon unfold over two consecutive days, with winners determined by their combined performance in all events. Performance is assessed using a points system for each event, not by the position achieved.

In modern track and field, the events for the men's decathlon are contested in the following order: 100 meters, long jump, shot put, high jump, 400 meters, 110-meter hurdles, discus throw, pole vault, javelin throw, and 1500 meters. The women's heptathlon comprises the following events in sequence: 100 meters hurdles, high jump, shot put, 200 meters, long jump, javelin throw, and 800 meters.

At the Olympics, the first combined events were men's competitions held at the 1904 Games in St. Louis, including a triathlon consisting of long jump, shot put, and 100-yard dash events. Additionally, a similar competition called an "all-around" debuted, first contested at the United States amateur championships in 1884. This all-around championship involved athletes competing in ten events, laying the groundwork for the decathlon. Although no combined events were held at 1908 Games, the 1912 Olympics introduced the modern decathlon event and a men's pentathlon, which lasted for only three Games. The inaugural women's combined event debuted in 1964 in the form of the pentathlon. This evolved to include two more disciplines, eventually becoming the heptathlon at the 1984 Olympics, reflecting the evolution of women's sports.

Two types of events take place on public roads—the marathon and race walking—both incredibly demanding and highly tactical, often leading to a variety of strategies with contestants sometimes even working together to outmaneuver a rival. Spectators gather along the route to watch and cheer on the athletes.

The <u>marathon</u> is a grueling long-distance foot race covering 42.195 kilometers (26 miles 385 yards), held as a road race. Participants can complete the marathon by running or using a run/walk strategy. Each year, over 800 marathons are organized worldwide, attracting a large number of recreational athletes, with some of the larger marathons hosting tens of thousands of participants.

When modern Olympics began in 1896, the initiators and organizers were looking for a widely appealing event to revive the spirit of ancient Greece. The marathon emerged as that key event and has become a major attraction, being refined later through the Olympic competition. The name "marathon" comes from the legend of a Greek messenger, who in 490 BC supposedly ran to Athens from the town of Marathon, Greece to carry the message of a Greek victory over the Persians.

In fact, the inaugural 1896 Olympic marathon course began in Marathon and concluded at Athens' Panathenaic Stadium, covering a distance of approximately 40 kilometers (25 miles). On April 10, 1896, Greek water-carrier Spyridon Louis clinched victory in the first Olympic marathon, completing the race in 2 hours, 58 minutes, and 50 seconds. The same route between Marathon and the Panathenaic Stadium was retraced when Athens hosted the Olympic Games again in 2004.

Initially, the race distance varied from 40 to 42 kilometers (25 to 26 miles) in the early editions, as it was typically based upon the distance between two points that the organizers felt were suitable. The marathon distance of 26 miles, 385 yards (42.195 kilometers) was established at the 1908 London Olympics, but it wasn't until the 1924 Paris Games that this distance became standard at the Olympics. The women's race was added to the program in 1984, at the Los Angeles Games.

It has become a tradition for the men's Olympic marathon to be the concluding event of the athletics calendar, held on the final day of the Games. This will change in 2024, with the women's marathon scheduled on the last day, while the men's race will take place a day earlier.

<u>Race walking</u> is a long-distance discipline within athletics. Although a foot race, it differs from running by requiring that one foot must appear to be in contact with the ground at all times. Furthermore, the athlete's knee of their advanced leg must not bend and the leg must straighten as the body passes over it. These rules are rigorously enforced by race judges throughout the event. If a race walker is shown three warnings from judges, it leads to disqualification of the athlete.

The sport originated from a British tradition of competitive long-distance walking known as *pedestrianism*, which began shaping the rules of the modern discipline around the mid-19th century. Compared to other forms of foot racing, race walkers have shorter stride lengths, necessitating a cadence comparable to world-class 800-1,500 meter runners to achieve competitive speeds.

Race walking for men made its Olympic debut in 1904 at St. Louis, but it was included as part of the "all-around championship", today's version of the decathlon. It first appeared as a standalone event at the 1908 Games, featuring a 3500-meter and a 10-mile race walk. A 10-kilometer version was introduced at the 1912 Olympics and it continued until 1952, with exceptions in 1928, 1932, and 1936. There was also a one-off 3000 meters walk at the 1920 Games.

The men's 20-kilometer walk became the standard short distance in 1956 and has remained so since. The longer 50-kilometer event for men was first held at the 1932 Olympics and was continuously included until the 2020 Games, with a brief absence in 1976. The first women's race walking event was introduced at the

1992 Olympics. Initially held over 10 kilometers, the women's event was extended to match the men's 20-kilometer distance from the 2000 Games onward.

Women have not commonly competed internationally in the 50-kilometer event, thus it was never considered for inclusion in the Olympic program. Consequently, it became the last event in Olympic athletics schedule in which men competed, while women did not have an equivalent. This will change in 2024, when a new marathon race walking mixed relay will replace the men's 50 kilometers. Notably, the 50-kilometer race stood out as the longest distance event at the Olympic Games.

In 2024, the athletics competitions will feature an equal number of medal events for men and women for the first time in Olympic history. A new addition to these Games is the marathon race walking mixed relay, replacing the men's 50 kilometers race walk. In this new event, twenty-five teams will participate, each consisting of one female and one male athlete. They will cover the marathon distance (42.195 kilometers) in four stages: male 11.45 km, female 10 km, male 10 km, and female 10.745 km.

Another change to the track and field program is the introduction of a repechage round format in all individual track events from 200 to 1500 meters and the hurdles events (110 for men, 100 for women, and 400 meters for both). This format provides runners with a second chance to enter the semifinal phase, replacing the previous system based on advancing through the fastest overall times (q) apart from those qualifying directly in the first-round heats (Q).

Road events (marathons and race walks) will take place in the morning session of the schedule, while all track, field and combined events will stage their finals in the evening session for the first time since London 2012. In its four-decade-long Olympic history, the women's marathon will occur on the last day of the athletics program for the first time, with the men's race scheduled a day before.

A total of **48 medal events** will be featured over eleven days, with 23 events each for women and men, along with 2 mixed events. Four venues will be used: Pont d'Iéna for race walking, Hôtel de Ville and Les Invalides for the start and end points of the marathon races, and Stade de France for the track and field events.

Finals contested on Thursday, 1st of August
- men's 20 km race walk at 07:30
- women's 20 km race walk at 09:20

Finals contested on Friday, 2nd of August
- men's decathlon (100 m, long jump, shot put, high jump, and 400 m)
- men's 10,000 m at 21:20

Finals contested on Saturday, 3rd of August
- men's shot put at 19:35
- women's triple jump at 20:20
- mixed 4 × 400 m relay at 20:55
- women's 100 m at 21:20
- men's decathlon (110 m hurdles, discus throw, pole vault, javelin throw, and 1500 m at 21:45)

Finals contested on Sunday, 4th of August
- women's high jump at 19:50
- men's hammer throw at 20:30
- men's 100 m at 21:55

Finals contested on Monday, 5th of August
- men's pole vault at 19:00
- women's discus throw at 20:30
- women's 5000 m at 21:10
- women's 800 m at 21:45

Finals contested on Tuesday, 6th of August
- women's hammer throw at 20:00
- men's long jump at 20:20
- men's 1500 m at 20:50
- women's 3000 m steeplechase at 21:10
- women's 200 m at 21:40

Finals contested on Wednesday, 7th of August
- mixed relay marathon race walk at 07:30
- women's pole vault at 19:00
- men's discus throw at 20:25
- men's 400 m at 21:20
- men's 3000 m steeplechase at 21:40

Finals contested on Thursday, 8th of August
- women's heptathlon (100 m hurdles, high jump, shot put, and 200 m)
- women's long jump at 20:00
- men's javelin throw at 20:25
- men's 200 m at 20:30
- women's 400 m hurdles at 21:25
- men's 110 m hurdles at 21:45

Finals contested on Friday, 9th of August
- women's 4 × 100 m relay at 19:30
- women's shot put at 19:40
- men's 4 × 100 m relay at 19:45
- women's 400 m at 20:00
- men's triple jump at 20:10
- women's heptathlon (long jump, javelin throw, and 800 m at 20:15)
- women's 10,000 m at 20:55
- men's 400 m hurdles at 21:45

Finals contested on Saturday, 10th of August
- men's marathon at 08:00
- men's high jump at 19:10
- men's 800 m at 19:25
- women's javelin throw at 19:40
- women's 100 m hurdles at 19:45
- men's 5000 m at 20:00
- women's 1500 m at 20:25
- men's 4 × 400 m relay at 21:12
- women's 4 × 400 m relay at 21:22

<u>Finals contested on Sunday, 11th of August</u>
- women's marathon at 08:00

Athletic contests in running, walking, jumping, and throwing are among the oldest sports, with roots tracing back to prehistoric times. Athletics events were depicted in Egypt as early as 2250 BC, with Asian civilizations also known to have encouraged athletics many centuries ago. The Tailteann Games, an ancient Celtic festival held in Ireland, featured running and stone-throwing among the sporting events during its thirty-day duration. The first ancient Olympics, held in 776 BC, featured the *stadion*, a stadium-length running event, as its original and only competition. This later expanded to include throwing and jumping events within the ancient pentathlon.

The modern development of the sport emerged mainly in the early 19th century. Organized amateur footraces were held in England as early as 1825, and the first competitions resembling today's track and field meets took place in 1840 in Shropshire, England. The sport saw substantial growth from 1860 onward. In 1861, the West London Rowing Club organized the first contest open to all amateurs, while the Amateur Athletic Club, founded in 1866, conducted the inaugural English championships. In North America, the first meet near Toronto occurred in 1839, but it was the establishment of the New York Athletic Club in the 1860s that solidified the sport's presence in the United States. Other championships began flourishing and spreading in the 1880s, particularly in England, the USA, and Europe.

Although track and field had gained a foothold in many countries by the late 1800s, it was not until the revival of the Olympic Games in 1896 that the sport become truly international. Despite its modest beginnings, the Olympics provided the inspiration and standardizing force, igniting global interest in track and field. In 1912, the international federation that oversees athletics competitions was established, further solidifying the sport's global reach.

It was a natural decision to include athletics, or track and field, at the inaugural Games of the modern Olympics held in 1896 in Athens, Greece. Its age-old position in the Olympic program makes this sport the crown jewel of the Summer Games. The men's events have remained unchanged since the 1932 Los Angeles Games, except for the addition of the 20-kilometer race walk at the 1956 Melbourne Games.

Women made their debut at the 1928 Olympics in Amsterdam, participating in five events: the 100, 800, 4×100 meters relay, high jump, and discus throw. Over the years, the women's competition expanded to seventeen events by 1992. With the inclusion of the 3000-meter steeplechase in 2008, female athletes now compete in the same number of events as their male counterparts. The only differences are that women participate in the heptathlon instead of the decathlon and the 100 rather than the 110 meters hurdles.

The 1960s witnessed a surge in athletics in developing countries, expanding the sport's global reach. At the Beijing 2008 Games, athletes from 62 countries competed in the finals, showcasing the sport's widespread participation and appeal.

In the medal standings, the USA has emerged as the dominant force in the competition, with 827 medals (344 gold, 269 silver, and 214 bronze). The former Soviet Union, with 193 medals (64 gold, 55 silver, and 74 bronze) and Great Britain, with 210 medals (55 gold, 83 silver, and 72 bronze), have also enjoyed considerable success in this sport at the Olympic Games.

TRAMPOLINE GYMNASTICS

The trampoline events feature athletes bouncing over 8 meters high in the air on a rectangular canvas made of synthetic fabric, known as a trampoline, as they execute acrobatic maneuvers. These can range from basic jumps in various positions like straight, pike, tuck, or straddle, to more complex combinations involving forward and/or backward somersaults and twists.

The trampoline bed is attached to a frame using steel springs, enabling athletes to achieve great height through its recoil action. Competitors perform routines consisting of ten elements, with each element scored based on its difficulty, execution, and time spent in the air. Points are deducted for poor form and deviation from the center of the trampoline bed. The sport is highly technical and requires absolute precision.

A total of 32 gymnasts (16 women and 16 men) will contest at Bercy Arena in **two medal events**:
- women's finals on Friday, August 2 at 13:50
- men's finals on Friday, August 2 at 19:45

Trampolining was invented in 1934 by George Nissen, an American gymnast who was inspired by circus acrobats performing on safety nets. He built the first prototype trampoline to recreate their acrobatics and used it to help enhance his own diving and tumbling skills. Initially serving as a training tool for astronauts and athletes in their related disciplines, the trampoline quickly became very popular as a sport in its own right. In the United States, trampolining was introduced into school physical education programs and found its way into private entertainment centers. Elsewhere in the world, the sport was most strongly adopted in Europe and the former Soviet Union. The inaugural trampoline world championships were organized in London in 1964, and 34 years later, the sport was formally integrated into the International Gymnastics Federation.

Trampoline became an Olympic sport at the Sydney Games in 2000, where men's and women's individual trampoline competitions were added to the other disciplines in the sport of gymnastics.

Although the first Olympic champions in this event were both from Russia, Irina Karavayeva and Alexander Moskalenko, China has dominated the sport and enjoys a significant lead in the trampoline medal table, having won 14 out of the 36 medals awarded so far. China also leads in the gold medal table, having won four out of the twelve to date.

The first and only athlete so far, male or female, to successfully defend their Olympic title (2012 and 2016) is Rosie MacLennan of Canada.

TRIATHLON

The mixed relay competition will return for its second appearance in the triathlon program, following its successful debut at the Tokyo Games, alongside the women's and men's individual events.

Triathlon is a multi-disciplinary endurance sport that combines swimming, cycling, and running into a single event. The race format at the Olympics for both the women's and men's events consist of a 1500-meter (0.93-mile) swim, a 40-kilometer (25-mile) cycle, and a 10-kilometer (6.2-mile) run. The competition consists of a single race without heats, where the first athlete to cross the finish line is the winner, a feat requiring versatility and skill.

As previously mentioned, the mixed relay event was added at the Tokyo 2020 Olympics. Teams of two men and two women compete in a relay format on a course consisting of a 300-meter (330-yard) swim, an 8-kilometer (5-mile) cycle, and a 2-kilometer (1.2-mile) run before tagging a teammate.

A total of 110 athletes will compete at Pont Alexandre III across **three medal events**:
- men's individual finals on Tuesday, July 30 at 08:00
- women's individual finals on Wednesday, July 31 at 08:00
- mixed relay finals on Monday, August 5 at 08:00

The evolution of triathlon as a distinct sport is difficult to trace with precision. Some consider events in early 20th-century France to be the beginnings of triathlon, with a competition that took place in 1920, known as *les trois sports*, involving a 3-kilometer run, a 12-kilometer bike ride, and a swim across the Marne River.

The first modern official triathlon race (swim/bike/run event) is considered the one held at San Diego in 1974. This event, named the Mission Bay Triathlon, featured an 8.5-kilometer (6.2 miles) run, an 8-kilometer (5 miles) cycle, and a swim just under 550 meters (500 yards). It was conceived and organized by Jack Johnstone and Don Shanahan, members of the San Diego Track Club. Neither of them had heard of the past French events and both believed their race was a unique idea.

Notable participants in this event were Judy and John Collins, who would go on to establish another major event in the history of triathlon. In 1978, they founded the Ironman Triathlon in Hawaii, comprising a 2.4-mile swim, an 112-mile bike ride, and a 26.2-mile run. This grueling event played a crucial role in promoting triathlon and inspiring athletes worldwide. The sport grew in popularity throughout the 1980s, and in 1989 the first world championships were held in Avignon, France.

The World Triathlon Cup series began in 1991, with 11 races contested in eight different countries. This series played a pivotal role in making the sport more accessible and popular. Consequently, it was included in the Olympics for the first time at the Sydney 2000 Games. As triathlon is a relatively new sport, no nation has emerged as a dominant force. Over the course of six Olympic Games so far, a total of 39 medals have been awarded, distributed among 16 countries. Great Britain leads with the highest number of gold medals won, although no nation has claimed more than three golds in total.

VOLLEYBALL

The volleyball tournaments at the 2024 Olympics are scheduled to run from July 27 to August 11 at South Paris Arena 1, part of the Paris Expo Porte de Versailles.

Volleyball is played by two teams of six players separated by a net, on an indoor rectangular court 18 meters long and 9 meters wide. The objective of the game is to score points by grounding the ball on the opposing team's side of the court or by causing the opposing team to commit a fault. The primary method of scoring involves players using their hands to "volley" the ball over the net, with each team being allowed up to three touches of the ball before it must be returned. The set is won by the first team to reach 25 points with a two-point margin, in a best-of-five sets format. If necessary, a fifth set is played to 15 points, still requiring a two-point margin for victory. For the first time in Olympic volleyball history, each participating team will have the option to include one additional athlete who won't actively compete, but can substitute for another player due to medical reasons. Consequently, team rosters will expand from 12 to 13 athletes.

Volleyball requires a combination of physical skills such as jumping, blocking, and spiking, as well as quick reflexes, especially with balls reaching speeds of up to 130 km/h, following a spectacular jump serve or smash. Teamwork and strategy are also essential elements of this sport.

A total of 24 teams (12 women's and 12 men's) will compete in **two medal events**:
- men's finals on Saturday, August 10 at 13:00
- women's finals on Sunday, August 11 at 13:00

William G. Morgan, a YMCA physical education director and a student at Springfield College, is credited with creating the game of volleyball in 1895 in Holyoke, Massachusetts. At the time, another indoor sport, basketball, was catching on in the area, having been invented just ten miles away in the city of Springfield, Massachusetts, only four years before. Originally named *mintonette*, volleyball was designed to be an indoor pastime, less rough than basketball, that could be enjoyed by older members of the YMCA. It drew inspiration from various sports, including baseball, tennis, and handball.

Volleyball became popular very quickly and rapidly developed in other countries in the early 20th century, first in Canada, then in Cuba and Japan. The first rulebooks for the sport were produced in the early 1900s and the inaugural international federation was established in 1947. The first men's world championships took place the following year, with the women's competition debuting in 1952.

Olympic volleyball's story began at the 1924 Paris Games, where it was featured as an unofficial exhibition event, highlighted by a one-time demonstration by the USA. Officially, volleyball made its Olympic debut at the Tokyo 1964 Games. Initially, both the women's and men's competitions followed a single round-robin format, where teams were grouped into a single pool and played each other once. This format persisted until the 1972 Games in Munich, when it transitioned to a combination of pool rounds followed by a knockout stage: quarter-finals, semi-finals, and finals to determine the medalists.

Teams from the Soviet Union and Cuba regularly found the Olympic podium in the 1980s, as did Italy and China in the 1990s, followed by Brazil in the 2000s. The former Soviet Union, Brazil, and the USA lead the Olympic volleyball standings, being the only three countries with at least ten medals each. The reigning Olympic champions in women's and men's are the USA and France, respectively.

WATER POLO

The water polo tournaments for the 2024 Games will take place from July 27 to August 11. Preliminary matches will take place at Paris Aquatic Center, with the final playoffs featured at the Paris La Défense Arena.

Water polo is an aquatic team sport played between two teams of seven players each. The dimensions officially approved for Olympic matches are 30×20 meter pool for men and 25×20 meter pool for women. The game takes place in an all-deep pool, preventing players from touching the bottom and consists of four eight-minute quarters. The objective is to score goals by throwing the ball into the opposing net.

Each team is made up of six field players and one goalkeeper. Excluding the goalkeeper, players are permitted to hold the ball with only one hand. Field players participate in both offensive and defensive roles during a game. They swim for positions around the pool, defend, execute passes and attempt shots at the goal while treading water. Possession lasts 30 seconds; if the team does not attack the goal within that time, possession passes to the opposing team.

Water polo is renowned for its physical demands and is often regarded as one of the most challenging sports to play. Strength, endurance, and physical prowess are crucial, complemented by teamwork, tactical thinking, and situational awareness, specific to team sports.

A total of 22 teams (10 women's and 12 men's) will compete in **two medal events**:
- women's finals on Saturday, August 10 at 15:35
- men's finals on Sunday, August 11 at 14:00

Water polo originated in England in the 19th century as a form of aquatic rugby. The game evolved from various water-based activities practiced in rivers and lakes. Early play was highly dangerous, as it allowed brute strength, wrestling, and holding opposing players underwater to recover the ball. The keeper stood outside the area and defended the goal by jumping in on any opponent trying to score.

In 1870s, the London Swimming Association developed a set of regulations for the sport to be used in indoor swimming pools. Later rules developed in Scotland emphasized a *soccer* (*European football*) style of play as opposed to the *rugby* variant. The game was first introduced in the United States in 1888. It featured the *rugby* style of play which looked like *American football* in the water. This "American style" of water polo became very popular by the late 1890's across the USA. However, the rest of the world adopted over time the Scottish-influenced rules, which formed the basis for the sport of water polo as we know it today.

The term *polo* comes from the English pronunciation of the Indian/Tibetan word *pulu*, which means ball. The first games were played with a ball made of India rubber.

Water polo has been part of the Olympics program since the second modern Games, in 1900 – first in the form of competitions between clubs, then tournaments between countries from 1908. It took a century for the women's event to be included in the Olympic Games.

Hungary has been the most successful country in men's tournament, with sixteen medals (including nine golds). On the other hand, the United States stands out as the only team to win multiple times in the women's tournament, capturing the gold in London 2012, Rio de Janeiro 2016, and Tokyo 2020. Italy is the first and only country so far to win both the men's and women's water polo tournaments.

WEIGHTLIFTING

Weightlifting is a sport in which athletes compete in raising a barbell loaded with weight plates from the ground to overhead, with the aim of successfully lifting the heaviest weights. It's a discipline driven as much by technique as raw strength, with athletes accustomed to lifting as much as twice and sometimes even three times their bodyweight.

There are two stages in modern Olympic weightlifting: the snatch and the clean and jerk.

In the snatch, the weightlifter picks up the barbell in a wide grip and lifts it above their head in one singular motion.

In the clean and jerk, the athlete is first required to pick up the barbell and bring it up to their chest (clean). The contestant must then pause and extend their arms and legs to lift it above the head (jerk) with straight elbows and hold it there until a buzzer is sounded.

In modern Olympic weightlifting, competitors are granted three attempts at both lifts, with the snatch performed first. The best result from each lift is combined to calculate the participant's overall score. The athlete achieving the highest total score is declared the winner. If two contestants have lifted the same combined weight, the one with the lower bodyweight is granted the advantage. Should the bodyweights also be equal, the one with fewer attempts will be the final winner.

A participant is allowed to increase the weight for their next attempt after a successful lift. The athlete who chooses to raise the lowest weight in the initial try is permitted to start the contest. They must make their lift within one minute of their name being called out. Weightlifters are allowed to use tape to cover parts of their body, such as the wrists and thumbs, to prevent injury. They also often rub chalk on their hands to make them dry before a lift, which prevents the barbell from slipping.

Weightlifting is a sport that requires exceptional physical strength as well as ironclad mental resolve to achieve great success in competitions.

Several changes are instituted in the weightlifting program for Paris, as the number of categories is reduced from fourteen in Tokyo to ten. Furthermore, a total of 120 athletes will compete in 2024, a substantial decrease from a full roster size of 196 at the previous Games.

A total of 120 weightlifters, equal split between men and women, will compete at South Paris Arena 6, part of the Paris Expo Porte de Versailles across the **ten medal events**:
- men's 61 kg finals on Wednesday, August 7 at 15:00
- women's 49 kg finals on Wednesday, August 7 at 19:30
- women's 59 kg finals on Thursday, August 8 at 15:00
- men's 73 kg finals on Thursday, August 8 at 19:30
- men's 89 kg finals on Friday, August 9 at 15:00
- women's 71 kg finals on Friday, August 9 at 19:30
- men's 102 kg finals on Saturday, August 10 at 11:30
- women's 81 kg finals on Saturday, August 10 at 16:00
- men's +102 kg finals on Saturday, August 10 at 20:30
- women's +81 kg finals on Sunday, August 11 at 11:30

Weightlifting—often known as Olympic weightlifting—has been around for thousands of years, yet the objective remains consistent: victory goes to the athlete who lifts the heaviest weight. Evidence of the sport dates to ancient civilizations such as Egypt and Greece, where people lifted heavy stones in contests of strength. Weightlifting re-emerged in the 19th century, when the inaugural world championships were held in 1891.

The sport featured at the first modern Olympic Games held in Athens in 1896, as part of the field events in track and field. There were two weightlifting events: lifting with one hand and lifting with two hands.

Although excluded from the Olympic program for several editions of the Games (1900, 1908, and 1912), weightlifting was reintroduced in 1920 at the Antwerp Games and has remained a fixture ever since.

The Olympic weightlifting program has greatly evolved over time. The one-hand event was dropped after the Paris 1924 Games and starting with the 1972 Munich Olympics, the clean and press – a variation of the clean and jerk with a three-step process, was discontinued due to difficulty in judging the techniques of weightlifters. Since the Montreal 1976 Games, there have been two lifts used in competition: the snatch and the clean and jerk.

Weight categories were first introduced at the 1920 Olympics, ranging from 60 to 82.5 kilograms. Over time, the number of classes and the weight limits for each class have changed several times. Notably, the lowest weight category disputed, 52 kilograms, made its debut at the 1972 Games in Munich. This edition also marked the introduction of the +110 kilograms, the highest weight category contested in Olympic weightlifting.

While the sport was reserved only for men at the Olympics, women's weightlifting competitions were first held at the Sydney 2000 Games.

At the beginning of the 20th century, European nations – particularly Germany, Austria, and France – dominated weightlifting. From the 1950s onward, Soviet athletes topped the podium until the 1990s, when athletes representing China, Türkiye, Greece, and Iran began to claim the majority of medals on offer. China has particularly excelled in women's weightlifting since its official introduction as an Olympic sport in 2000.

In the medal standings, the former Soviet Union leads with 62 medals (39 gold, 21 silver, and 2 bronze), followed closely by China, also with 62 medals (38 gold, 16 silver, and 8 bronze) and the USA with 44 medals (16 gold, 17 silver, and 11 bronze).

Among male weightlifters, Greece's Pyrros Dimas stands out as the most successful Olympian, securing three gold medals and a bronze across different weight categories throughout the years. Another Greek weightlifter, Akakios Kakiasvilis, as well as Türkiye's Halil Mutlu and Naim Suleymanoglu and China's Lü Xiaojun, have also captured three Olympic golds each.

Chen Yanqing, representing China, Chinese Taipei's Hsu Shu-ching and Rim Jong-sim from North Korea are the most successful women weightlifters at the Olympics, having won two gold medals.

WRESTLING

The wrestling competitions at the 2024 Olympics in Paris are scheduled to run from August 5 to 11 at Grand Palais Éphémère in *Champ de Mars*. Men will compete in both freestyle and Greco-Roman categories, while women will only participate in freestyle wrestling.

There are two Olympic wrestling disciplines, each with its own rules. In Greco-Roman wrestling, a competitor can only use his arms and upper body to attack his opponent above the waist. Freestyle wrestling is a much more open form of the sport in which competitors also use their legs and can hold opponents above or below the waist.

Nevertheless, the objective is the same in both styles. Contested on a circular combat area 9-meter in diameter, a bout consists of two three-minute periods each, with a 30-second break in between. Wrestlers must either use their bare hands to pin their opponent's two shoulders down to the mat without holding them by their singlet (this is called a 'fall') or, if no fall is secured during the bout, have the most points at the end of regulation time by performing takedown and reversal moves.

Each division features sixteen wrestlers engaging in a single-elimination tournament. A repechage system is used to determine the winners of two bronze medals. The two finalists contend for gold and silver medals, while those defeated by the finalists enter the repechage. Competitors who lost in the first round or quarterfinals against a finalist face off, with winners advancing to a bronze medal match against semifinal losers. The process is repeated for each finalist, resulting in two separate bronze medal matches.

A total of 288 wrestlers (192 men and 96 women) are expected to compete across **eighteen medal events** in different weight categories:
- men's greco-roman 60 kg finals on Tuesday, August 6 at 19:55
- men's greco-roman 130 kg finals on Tuesday, August 6 at 20:30
- women's freestyle 68 kg finals on Tuesday, August 6 at 21:15
- men's greco-roman 77 kg finals on Wednesday, August 7 at 19:55
- men's greco-roman 97 kg finals on Wednesday, August 7 at 20:30
- women's freestyle 50 kg finals on Wednesday, August 7 at 21:15
- men's greco-roman 67 kg finals on Thursday, August 8 at 19:55
- men's greco-roman 87 kg (finals on Thursday, August 8 at 20:30
- women's freestyle 53 kg finals on Thursday, August 8 at 21:15
- men's freestyle 57 kg finals on Friday, August 9 at 19:55
- men's freestyle 86 kg finals on Friday, August 9 at 20:30
- women's freestyle 57 kg finals on Friday, August 9 at 21:15
- men's freestyle 74 kg finals on Saturday, August 10 at 19:55
- men's freestyle 125 kg finals on Saturday, August 10 at 20:30
- women's freestyle 62 kg finals on Saturday, August 10 at 21:15
- men's freestyle 65 kg finals on Sunday, August 11 at 12:25
- men's freestyle 97 kg finals on Sunday, August 11 at 13:00
- women's freestyle 76 kg finals on Sunday, August 11 at 13:45

Wrestling is one of the oldest sports in human history—possibly the oldest. Multiple sculptures, reliefs, and cave drawings—some of which date to around 15,000 years ago—show wrestlers using various holds that are still used in the present-day sport. Having been contested across civilizations like ancient Mesopotamia, Egypt, India, China, and Greece, wrestling was a key part of the ancient Olympic Games, where it was first contested in 708 BC. Wrestling matches were organized as its own event in two disciplines ('upright' - *orthe palé* and 'ground' - *kato palé*) as well as part of the pentathlon.

Modern wrestling consists of two disciplines: Greco-Roman, rooted in the ancient tradition, and freestyle, a more contemporary format.

Wrestling has been contested at every modern Summer Olympic Games, except Paris 1900. Greco-Roman wrestling debuted at the Olympics in 1896 and has been a permanent fixture since 1908, exclusively for men. The Greco-Roman wrestling competition in 1896 was a unified contest without any weight class divisions, with the first recorded champion being Germany's Carl Schumann. Remarkably, Schumann also won three gymnastics events at the Athens Games that year. In those days, winners received silver medals with olive branches. The tradition of gold medals only started in 1904.

Traditionally, dominant nations in Greco-Roman wrestling at the Olympics include the former Soviet Union, Sweden, Finland, Hungary, Türkiye, Bulgaria, and Romania.

Freestyle wrestling made its debut at the St. Louis 1904 Games with only local wrestlers from the United States participating. It was also the first time in Olympic history where weight category events were introduced. Freestyle wrestling was taken off schedule for the 1912 Games, but made a return in the 1920 edition and has been a permanent fixture since. Women's competitions were introduced at the Athens Games in 2004.

Success in Olympic freestyle wrestling has been achieved by countries such as the United States, Japan, the former Soviet Union, Türkiye, Sweden, Finland, Bulgaria, and Iran.

Wrestlers representing the Soviet Union have won a total of 116 medals at the Games, with 62 of those being gold. Team USA athletes have secured 142 medals, including 57 golds. Japan stands out as the most successful nation in women's wrestling at the Games, claiming 15 out of a possible 24 gold medals.

Individually, Cuba's Mijain Lopez (2008-2020) and Japan's Kaori Icho (2004-2016) are the most successful Olympic wrestlers in the modern era, each with four gold medals. In 2016, Icho made history as the first woman in any sport to win individual gold in the same discipline at four consecutive Olympics.

All times listed are in Paris time (Central European Summer Time), except for surfing competitions.

REFERENCES

https://olympics.com/

https://www.worldaquatics.com/

https://worldathletics.org/

https://www.worldarchery.sport/

https://www.gymnastics.sport/site/

https://bwfbadminton.com/

https://www.fiba.basketball/

https://www.worlddancesport.org/

https://www.canoeicf.com/

https://www.uci.org/

https://www.fei.org/

https://fie.org/

https://www.fifa.com/

https://www.igfgolf.org/

https://www.ihf.info/

https://www.fih.hockey/

https://www.ijf.org/

https://www.uipmworld.org/

https://worldrowing.com/

https://www.world.rugby/

https://www.sailing.org/

https://www.issf-sports.org/

https://www.worldskate.org/

https://www.ifsc-climbing.org/

https://isasurf.org/

https://www.ittf.com/

https://www.itftennis.com/

http://www.worldtaekwondo.org/

https://www.triathlon.org/

https://www.fivb.com/

https://beta.iwf.sport/

https://uww.org/

Thank you for reading! If you found this guide helpful, we'd love to hear your feedback in a review. Enjoy the Olympic Games!